# Introducing
# DESIGN
## Technology Across the Curriculum

LIVIHBEC

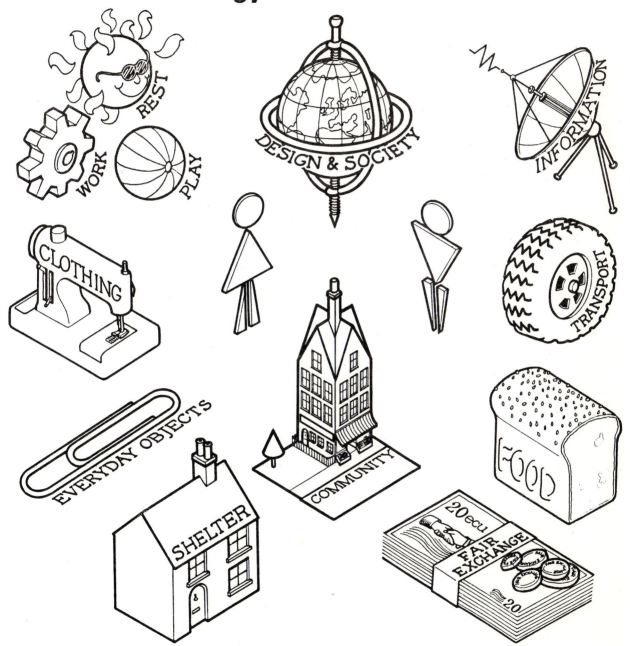

## Tristram Shepard

**Hutchinson**

London   Melbourne   Sydney   Auckland   Johannesburg

Hutchinson Education

An imprint of
Century Hutchinson Ltd
62–65 Chandos Place
London WC2N 4NW

Century Hutchinson
Australia Pty Ltd
89–91 Albion Street, Surry Hills
New South Wales 2010, Australia

Century Hutchinson
New Zealand Limited
PO Box 40-086, Glenfield
Auckland 10, New Zealand

Century Hutchinson
South Africa (Pty) Ltd
PO Box 337, Bergvlei
2012 South Africa

First published 1989

Designed and illustrated by
Tristram Ariss
**Cartoons by Nathan Ariss**

Set in 11 on 12pt Rockwell
by Avocet Robinson, Buckingham

Printed in Great Britain by
Scotprint Ltd, Musselburgh,
Scotland

**British Library Cataloguing in
Publication Data**
Shepard, Tristram
    Introducing design: technology
    across the curriculum.
    1. Design. For schools
    I. Title
    745.4

ISBN 0–09–172976–9

For Tricia, Jane and Simon

## Acknowledgements

I would like to thank the following people for their contributions:

Departmental staff from Simon Langton Boys' School, Canterbury:
Martyn Dukes, Brian Hurlow, Gill Kendall, Loraine Moore and
Evie Safarewicz

Philip Poole for his initial exploration of the desert island and
Robert Weinberg for his cartoon on page 55

Eileen Adams, Ken Baynes and Krysia Brochocka for their support and
encouragement

Last, but by no means least, all past and present pupils of
Simon Langton Boys' and Girls' Schools whose considerable
achievements are illustrated here: they continue to delight and inspire
us with their ideas, enthusiasm and the outstanding quality of their work.

Tristram Shepard
Canterbury, August 1988

The following extracts are reproduced with permission:
page 5 from *Launchpad*, Science Museum;
page 55 *The Domestic Help* by Adrian Henry from *The Phantom
Lollipop Lady and Other Poems*, © 1986 Methuen Children's Books;
page 87 adapted from *Future Shock* by Alvin Toffler, The Bodley Head.

The author and publisher are grateful to the following for permission to
reproduce photographs:

Cover/18  Robert Harding Picture
          Library
       11  Ford Motor Co Ltd
       16  Rene Magritte 'The False
          Mirror'. Oil on canvas (54 x
          80.9cm). Collection, Museum
          of Modern Art, New York. Purchase
       17  Ace Photo Agency
       29  Stephen Scoffham,
          Canterbury Urban Studies Centre
    30/31  Eileen Adams. 'Learning
          Through Landscapes' Project
       32  1) Lucien Herve, 2) Milton
          Keynes Development Corporation
       34  1) North Thames Gas Board
          2) Lincoln Museum
          3) Colchester and Essex Museum
          4) Science Museum, London
       35  Kenwood Ltd
       41  Mary Evans Picture Library
       45  BBC Books
       47  Sony (UK) Ltd
       53  TeleFocus (British Telecom)
       62  Hutchison Library
       63  1) John Donat, 2) Peter Cook
       67  1) The Walt Disney Company
          2) Stephen Moreton-Prichard
          3) Architectural Association
       68  Gerald Duckworth & Co. Ltd
       78  Rowntree Mackintosh PLC
       79  Sealink (British Ferries Ltd)
       84  1) TeleFocus (British Telecom)
          2) British Airports Authority

    86/87  Mary Evans Picture Library
       88  Tony Duffy, All Sport
          Photographic Ltd
       89  Cooper Canada Ltd
       90  Mary Evans Picture
          Library/Alan R Smith, Barnaby's
          Picture Library/British Aerospace
       97  'Fashion and Surrealism' at
          the V&A's Twentieth Century
          Gallery, Summer 1988.
          Exhibition produced by
          Garth Hall. Associates,
          designed by Brian Griggs.
          First shown at the Fashion
          Institute of Technology, New
          York. Accompanying
          publication by Richard
          Martin, published by Thames
          and Hudson
       98  Portrait of Rudolph II as
          Vertumnus by Guiseppe
          Archimboldo, Skokloster
          Slott, Sweden
      103  Museum of the Moving
          Image, London
      104  N.A.S.A./Science Photo Library
      105  International Centre for
          Conservation Education
          Photo Library
      106  1) Tim Davis, Science Photo Library
          2) I.C.C.E. Photo Library
      107  I.C.C.E. Photo Library
      111  N.A.S.A.

Other photographs by Tim Fagan and Tristram Shepard.

# Contents

**4   Introduction**
4    Have you ever ...?
4    Taking the initiative
5    What is design? What is
      technology?
6    Survival in a technological
      world

**7   Design skills**
8    Evaluation
9    Asking questions/
      investigation
10   Developing ideas of your
      own
12   Realization
13   Planning and organization
14   Presentation
16   Imagination

**18   Shipwrecked!**
20   Survival
25   Rescue

**26   Everyday products,
       places and
       communications**

**28   Community**
29   Environmental evaluation
30   Schoolscapes
32   City centre community
33   Local issues
33   Planning your own city

**34   Everyday objects**
35   Human factors
36   Product evaluation
37   Nice and nasty
39   Everyday objectivity
40   A museum of design
41   Fantastic inventions
42   Hidden uses

**44   Fair exchange**
45   Commercial break
47   Listening in
52   Soap opera

**53   Work, rest and play**
54   Job centre
55   The domestic help
56   Robomotion
58   Fun machines
59   Joyful noises
60   Fun and games

**62   Shelter**
62   Home sweet home
64   My house
67   All change

**72   Information**
73   Communication evaluation
74   Person to person
76   It's not what you say ...
77   Am I making myself clear?
77   Mind over matter
77   Communication
      breakdown
78   Symbols and logos

**80   Transport**
80   Getting around
81   Saver return
82   Terminus
84   Holiday exchange
85   Airport survival kit
85   On the run
86   Legoids
87   Increasing speed

**88   Clothing**
89   Clothes sense
89   Fit for the job
90   Off the peg
92   Roboritual
97   Any colour you like
97   Fantastic hats

**98   Food**
99   Rational diets
99   Gastronomic guesswork
99   Designer spells
100  Back to nature
102  Fast food
103  Sandwich survey
103  Guess who's coming to the
      party?

**104  Design and society**
104  Spaceship Earth
108  A campaign of action
109  Futurehome 2000
110  Moonbase: a giant leap for
      mankind?

**112  Index**

# Introduction

These introductory pages help to explain more about **design** and **technology**, and provide a useful reference guide to the **design skills** you will need to complete the various assignments.

The first main section is intended to increase your awareness of the way in which **people** have come to depend on technology for their **survival**. You will find yourself shipwrecked on a remote desert island without any sophisticated technology to make life easy.

After you have been rescued, the rest of the text and design assignments in each section of the book will invite you to consider and explore the technological advantages, disadvantages and possibilities of modern **products**, **places** and **communications**. For good or bad, technology is here to stay, and will continue to change the way we live.

The final section is about the long-term survival of our planet as a whole. Like the desert island, the natural resources of the Earth are limited: in order to maintain its finely balanced natural systems we must think very carefully about the way we use our present technological capability.

What sort of future world do **you** want to live in?

## Have you ever ...?

Have you ever:
- made someone a birthday card?
- played with a construction set?
- moulded some clay or Plasticine?
- made a sand castle?
- furnished a dolls' house?
- made a model village?
- written and performed a play?
- organized a party?
- written a computer program?
- made things from cardboard boxes?
- organized a secret club or society?

If so, then you have already gained some very valuable experiences in the processes of designing. All the activities above will have probably involved you in:
- taking the initiative to do something worthwhile
- thinking about and deciding what needed to be done and when
- choosing and using materials and simple tools
- trying things out and changing them if they were not right
- discussing ideas and actions with other people.

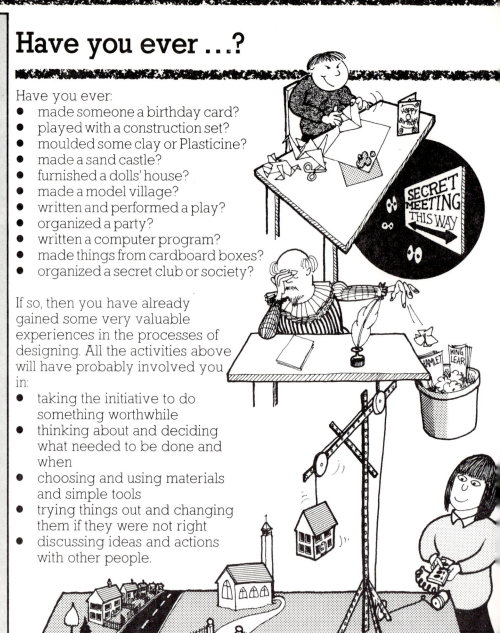

## Taking the initiative

You may well find the assignments in this book very different to most of the other activities you are asked to do at school. Just sitting at the back of the class, waiting to be told exactly what to do and when, isn't going to get you very far.

It is up to you to make your own individual contribution to what is going on. Don't hesitate to make suggestions about the best way to proceed, or to discuss a particular direction which you think might be interesting to explore.

When you come up against a problem, don't expect your teacher to immediately know all the right answers. Every situation is slightly different, and your particular problem, and the way you decide to go about solving it, will need an individual approach.

Try and see your teacher as more of a guide than an instructor. Be ready to carefully explain what you have discovered through your research, what ideas you've had and so on. Listen carefully to the suggestions which are made, and try them out to see if they are any help.

# What is design? What is technology?

During the past ten years or so the word **design** has become very fashionable. Everyone has heard of 'designer clothes', for example, and there is a growing range of other everyday products – like pens, personal stereos, torches, etc. – which are very clearly intended to look as though their visual appearance has been 'designed' by someone.

And what about **technology**? Again it is a word we hear often these days, and most people immediately think either of microchips, laser beams and fibre optics, or of complex machines and devices, such as motor cars, aeroplanes and space rockets.

In fact these are rather limited descriptions. Design involves a great deal more than just choosing the latest styles, and technology goes a lot further than knowing how things work.

Technology can be simple and straightforward as well as very complex, because absolutely everything humans produce, from a paperclip to a space station, has at some point been designed. Many people take technological decisions every day without even realizing it.

Most people tend to use the words design and technology to mean slightly different things in different situations, which can be a bit confusing at times.

In fact the two words have very similar meanings and uses – one could often be substituted for the other. You might find it useful though to remember the following general descriptions:

- **Technology** usually refers to all manufactured materials, machines, devices and systems which help people to extend their capabilities in order to survive more easily and effectively.

- **Designing** is the creative process of using or adapting technology to provide the things people need or want. It involves identifying things which are needed, developing possible ideas, and making them happen.

- **Good design** occurs when the technology which has been created is successful in improving the quality of life for a human being.

You may have subjects on your timetable called 'art and design' and 'craft, design and technology' However, you will soon discover that many of the assignments in this book also involve activities you do in English, maths, science, geography, history, drama and home economics.

Just as you need to use words and numbers in all your work, design and technology are a common dimension of virtually everything you do. In tackling the assignments in this book you will need to draw freely and frequently from most of the other subjects you are doing in school, and from many things you do outside school.

## Technology and us

What are the important parts of a person? Here are three of them:

you have a *body*, with muscles and arms and legs, so that you can move about, get food and make things;

you have a *brain*, which you use to remember and imagine things, and work out what you need to do;

finally you have *senses*, like seeing and hearing, so that you can find out what is going on around you, and communicate with other people.

You can do quite a lot with your body, brain and senses.

Without any help at all, most of us can jump a stream a metre wide, remember a list of three or four things to buy when we go shopping, and shout a message to someone 50 metres away.

But for harder tasks we need help, and that's where technology comes in. With the help of a rope, we can swing across a wider river. With pencil and paper we can write a long shopping list and take it with us. With a mirror we can flash a message to someone many kilometres away. The rope, the pencil and paper and the mirror are all things that help us – simple technology helping us do more than we can do with body, brain and senses alone.

Today, there seems hardly any limit to what we can do with the help of technology. We can 'jump' across an ocean by aeroplane. We can 'remember' millions of words and pictures with a video recorder. And we can 'talk' to people the other side of the world by telephone.

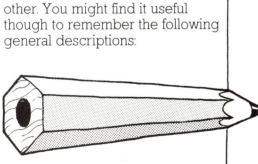

# Survival in a technological world

In order to survive physically, there are certain basic things human beings need – air, food and water. Meanwhile some form of clothing and shelter helps protect us from the extremes of weather, and health care assists when our bodies fail us in some way.

At the same time we also have many important emotional survival needs which need to be provided for – love, security, a sense of purpose and identity, the ability to learn, and so on.

Without these basic life-support systems we would be unable to survive for very long. As well as helping to provide these essentials, technology also serves to enhance them, by making things easier to obtain, and more plentiful.

Today, most of us live in a warm, secure **shelter** – a house, usually in a **community** we can feel a part of. **Transport** gets us where we want to go quickly and safely. Modern **information technology** systems inform us rapidly about what is going on in the world.

A wide range of sophisticated **everyday objects** gets things done more effectively. Our **work** is more organized and efficient, our **rest** more relaxing and our **play** more stimulating. **Food** is plentiful and convenient and our **clothing** is light, bright and easy to clean. Goods and services are carefully marketed to ensure we obtain a **fair exchange** for our money.

But the world is based on the idea of balance. Technology brings disadvantages as well as advantages. Many of us have become obsessed with trying to obtain more and more physical comfort at the expense of our emotional needs. And also, because of that obsession, we are using up the natural resources of our planet far too quickly.

We often marvel at the cleverness of some new invention, but sometimes forget to ask if it really helps us. Design and technology are as much about **people** as they are about **machines**, **devices** and **systems**.

If we are to continue to survive we need to achieve a better balance between what we actually need and how much we just want, and between our short-term profit and our long-term happiness.

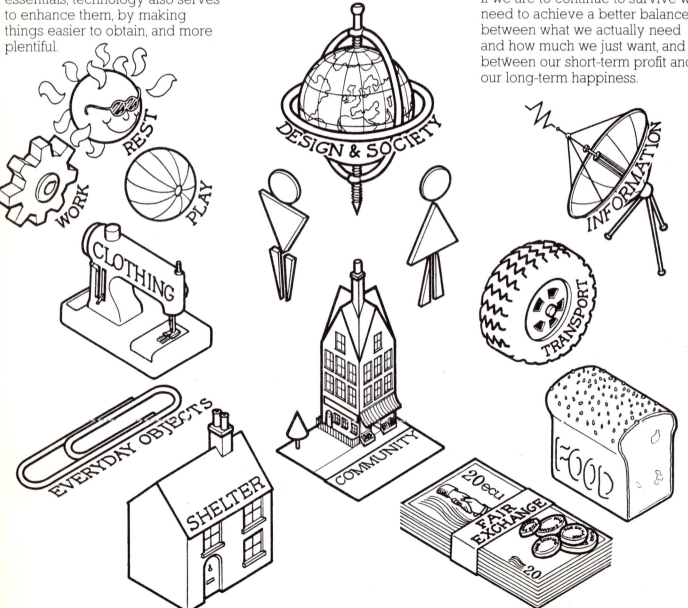

# Design skills

In order to successfully create the things which people need and want using the capabilities of technology, some **design skills** are required.

In one sense the processes of designing are not very difficult, but do require the application of a lot of very different activities. It certainly all takes a great deal of time and effort.

**Evaluating** how well things work is very important, as is the ability to **plan and organize** what you do as your design ideas progress.

Some **investigation** is always necessary to find out more about what is needed. Thinking up and **developing ideas of your own**, and choosing the best possible solution, are other essential ingredients.

This often involves making and testing **prototypes** of some sort, and then committing yourself to some form of final **realization**. Ingenious solutions are not a great deal of use unless they can be effectively explained to other people, so communication or **presentation** is vital as well.

Finally, successful designing requires the use of the **imagination** to think and feel about how things could be. Without our imaginations we would not be able to create and explore our visions of how we would like to live

Each of the various assignments in this book will give you the opportunity to use different mixtures and measures of all the full range of design skills.

**Keeping a project diary**

A project diary is an excellent way of recording and summarizing how well your work is progressing. If you can, spend the last few minutes of every lesson keeping it up to date, or complete it at home on the same day.

Try and make it more than just a factual account by adding in comments to indicate how you feel about how things are going. Aim to explain clearly any decisions you have made and how and why you took them. Don't forget to add simple illustrations whenever possible.

Thursday 15th
I made good progress with the development of my ideas today. I thought up several ways in which I could link the main parts together. I also realized that I need to find out more about how much it will cost.

During the next two weeks I must test my ideas out. My teacher was pleased with my

And so to be

# Evaluation ⚖

An important design skill to develop is the ability to make judgements about things – how well they work, how they could be more effective. You will often find yourself having to consider these sorts of things as you work through an assignment.

There are lots of useful words which can help make your evaluations easier and more effective. A selection of them is provided here. Find out the meanings of any you don't know, and try using them all more in your work.

bright · HEAVY · ugly · clumsy · Bulky · Bold · GLOSSY · weak · dull · Neat · SOLID · fussy · FRAGILE · DURABLE · DECORATIVE · delicate · MODERN · CONTRASTING · brittle · IMPRESSIVE · ROBUST · unified

## Evaluating the things you are designing

As you are developing your own design ideas you will often need to ask yourself:
- which are your most promising ideas?
- how well do they solve the problems involved?
- what needs further development?
- how could your ideas be improved?

## Evaluating the way you are designing something

You will have to consider whether or not you are:
- doing enough research work?
- considering a wide enough range of possible solutions?
- testing your ideas out sufficiently?
- making your final realization as clear and well produced as it can be?
- planning and organizing your work properly?
- being persistent enough?

## Evaluating your own progress

You will need to think carefully about:
- what areas of thinking and doing you are making most progress in
- what your particular strengths are
- what your weaknesses are
- what other people say about your work.

A **final evaluation** at the end of your project is also very important.

## Evaluating existing products, places and communications

It is often necessary to make judgements about the quality of things which already exist. By doing so we can assess which is the best or worst, and whether there is a need to develop a more satisfactory solution. These are dealt with in more detail on pages 29 (environmental evaluation), 36 (product evaluation) and 73 (communication evaluation).

rough · smooth · AWKWARD · HARSH · (subtle)

COLOURFUL

## ASSESSMENT CHECKLIST

Through the notes and comments you make your teacher should be able to assess how well you have developed your ability to evaluate:
- ☐ existing products, places and communications
- ☐ the things you design and the way you design them
- ☐ the effort and progress you have made.

Whenever you tackle any of the assignments in this book you will need to start asking some questions, such as:

- Why ...?
- When ...?
- How much ...?
- What ...?
- How ...?
- Why not ...?
- Where ...?

Some of the questions are provided for you, but there will always be more that you need to think out for yourself.

The next stage is to try and discover some answers to your questions, and that involves doing some **research** – finding out about things for yourself. Your teacher may provide you with some of the information you will need, but often it will be up to you.

This shouldn't be too difficult, however, because most of the answers can be discovered:

- at home
- in your neighbourhood
- at a local youth club or leisure centre
- in a local library
- in school.

Often you will need to **ask** other people for information – not strangers of course, but your family, relatives and friends. Sometimes you will need to **watch** these people to find out how they set about doing certain tasks.

Of course you may already know some of the information which is required, but perhaps you will also need to refer to particular books or magazines.

Sometimes the information you discover will be **factual** – how big something is, how fast it goes, how much it cost, etc., and sometimes the information will be a matter of **opinion** – what people think and feel about things, their likes and dislikes, what is important to them, and so on.

## What you think you might want...

Latest model cam-corder

Designer shades

A look of grim determination

Portable word-processor

Full set of technical pens

Auto wind autofocus camera

Extra lenses, films, filters

Designer flask for endless cups of coffee

Your ears to listen to the things people tell you about

Your eyes to observe what people do

Your mouth to ask questions, say please and thankyou, and to smile as often as possible

A pen, pencil and sketch pad

A simple camera and/or audio cassette recorder can also be useful

## All you actually need

Most of your research will have to be done early on in your project, though quite often you will need to do some more later if you discover something important you need to know.

Don't forget that it is very important that you make a record of all the information you discover. This work should be fairly neat and easy for your teacher to follow. Try to use a good mixture of words and visual material such as sketches, plans, diagrams, charts, etc.

## ASSESSMENT CHECKLIST

Your teacher will want to assess how well you've set about doing your research work. You are likely to gain credit if you can show that you have:
- ☐ used your initiative to find out things for yourself
- ☐ undertaken more than one research activity
- ☐ obtained a mixture of facts and opinions
- ☐ recorded your findings in detail, neatly and using illustrations as well as words.

# Developing ideas of your own (1)

To complete any of the assignments in this book you will have to be willing to have your own thoughts and ideas about things you are asked to design. This is not as difficult as it sounds, providing you remember that at this stage it doesn't matter if you make mistakes or suggestions which sound a bit crazy at first. No one will be expecting you to come up with brilliant ideas straight away!

WATT AN IDEA!

## First thoughts

Very few ideas could be said to be totally new and original, so don't worry if yours aren't either. Many famous inventions came about as a result of someone taking an existing idea and transforming it in some way – changing some of the details or using it in a different way to serve a new purpose.

Never be content with just your first idea. Think up and make a note of a whole range of possibilities and then choose the best one. The most successful ideas seem to come to us as a sudden flash of inspiration, but only if we have already spent a lot of time struggling to solve the problem.

Remember to record all your ideas and decisions at this stage using a mixture of sketches and words.

## Developing the details

In most of the assignments it will be best to start by working on paper, but eventually you will usually need to make a simple **prototype** of some sort to help you transform and develop your ideas into further detail.

Think of a prototype as something you can test out in some way to check that you haven't made any disastrous mistakes. First decide exactly what it is that you want to test – for example:
- Is it large enough?
- Is it the right colour?
- Will it work?

Then think about what sort of prototypes you will need to make to test those things out most effectively

For example, your prototypes may or may not need to be smaller or bigger than the real thing. And would it be better to make it in a different material which is easier and quicker to work, or cheaper perhaps?

As always it is extremely important that you keep a very careful record of all the ideas you have, so don't throw any of your sketches or notes away, and don't make them so rough that no one else can follow them.

Have you tried making your idea:

taller   lighter   longer   shorter   wider   darker   sideways   upside down   back to front   bigger   smaller   inside OUT   backwards

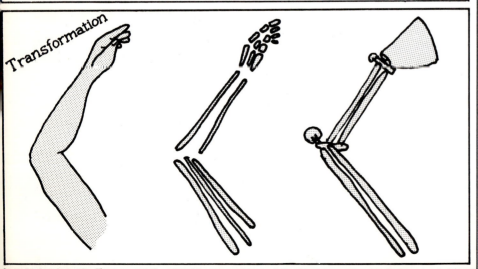

Transformation

## ASSESSMENT CHECKLIST

Your teacher will be looking for evidence that you have tried to develop some ideas of your own. To make this convincing, try and remember to always:
- [ ] come up with several possible answers
- [ ] experiment by transforming previous ideas
- [ ] make at least one prototype, having thought carefully about what needs to be tested and the best way to do it
- [ ] record all your ideas and decisions in full.

## Case study

Design involves a great deal more than taking the first pieces of material you find and knocking them together any old how.

The designers of the Ford Sierra began work with an extensive market-research programme, and much general discussion about the sort of car which was needed.

Their ideas were then developed in detail through the use of a wide range of prototypes. Each one enabled them to test and evaluate a different aspect of the final design.

The whole process, from initial concept decisions to public unveiling, took over four years.

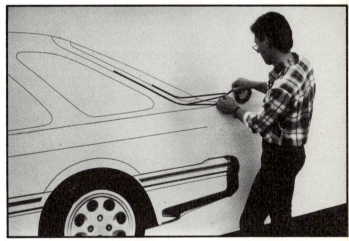

# Realization ✋

Brilliant ideas are of little value unless they can be brought into some sort of reality and communicated to other people.

There are many ways of achieving this, and each assignment will need a slightly different approach. Sometimes you will be directed towards the production of a particular drawing, model or other representation of your ideas, but it is largely up to you to decide which method will be the most effective.

Often a combination of written and graphic presentations and three-dimensional models will be needed to fully explain:
● what your task was
● what your proposed idea is
● how it would work
● why it would be effective
● which areas would need further development.

You will also need to consider exactly who you are trying to communicate this information to and think about:
● how much they already know
● how much they need to know
● how they might react to your ideas.

Your final statements might involve one, or more probably a mixture, of the following:
● scale, or full-size construction(s) in any appropriate materials
● two-dimensional graphic work (sketches, measured drawings, diagrams, photographs, etc.)
● video or audio tapes, computer programs or images
● paintings, drawings, prints, etc.
● performance (drama, movement, costume, music, etc.)
● creative writing
● formal written reports.

All this will take some time to decide on and to plan out in detail. You may well have to start by doing roughs of final drawings, or practise making certain parts before tackling a complicated model, or rehearsing a spoken presentation. As always make sure you keep any notes or other evidence of your thinking.

And remember that whatever form your final realization takes it will be most important to work on it as accurately and carefully as possible.

## ASSESSMENT CHECKLIST

For assessment purposes, make sure you have covered the following:
☐ a careful selection of the best ways of realizing your ideas
☐ choosing the most appropriate materials and ways of working with them
☐ achieving the best standard of workmanship you can manage.

# Planning and organization

Learning how to plan and organize your time and resources as effectively as possible is essential if your assignments are to be successfully completed.

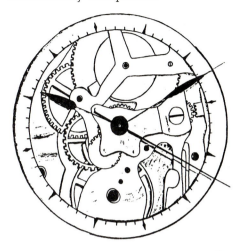

"Time waits for no one"

"More haste, less speed"

"Never put off till tomorrow what can best be done today"

## Time

Your teacher will usually tell you how long you have to complete a particular activity, and probably how long to spend on each stage, which could range from ten minutes to several weeks.

You will nearly always find that there never seems to be enough time to do things as well as you would like to, which is why it is important to learn to use the available time as effectively as possible.

Leaving everything until the last moment is not a good idea. Finding out about things takes time – particular books are not always immediately available, and people who need to be interviewed may be busy.

Our best ideas seem to come while we are not directly concentrating on that particular aspect of our work, so the night before isn't really long enough to let our minds explore the possibilities.

And preparing complex presentation drawings, models or performances can be the most time-consuming activity of all. Always start well in advance as most things will take longer than expected. There's never time to sit around doing nothing waiting for the glue to dry – there are always other parts of the project to attend to.

## Resources

Most of the special drawing equipment, workshop tools and materials you are going to need will probably be provided for you at school. However there may be some special items which you could usefully remember to bring in from home, though do ask permission first. And if you have been asked to do some preparatory work at home, don't forget that either – it will be needed for reference in class.

## Getting back on target

If you do find yourself getting behind for any reason at all, then you must do something to ensure that you do still manage to finish on time. As a general rule it is usually better to have something 'not as good as might have been' completed, than it is to have a 'great idea' which you haven't got round to testing or presenting.

Keep a careful check on how much longer you have to complete the work and set yourself a series of shorter-term targets to ensure you will make it on time.
- What could least noticeably be left out?
- What could be best left in rough form?
- Which are the most essential parts to complete fully?

Of course you might find yourself with the opposite problem when it looks as if you are going to finish long before anyone else. If this happens you should check that you have covered each previous stage thoroughly enough and haven't rushed things. Maybe you can spend any extra time refining your ideas and the way in which you intend to present them.

## ASSESSMENT CHECKLIST

Your teacher will need to be able to see that you have:
- [ ] planned ahead wisely
- [ ] not left everything to the last possible moment
- [ ] remembered to complete and bring in any work which needs to be done at home
- [ ] finished your project exactly on time.

# Presentation (1)

The way in which you present **all** your work is extremely important – not just the final realization, but the preparatory stages too. On these two pages are a series of simple tips to help you develop the way you present your two-dimensional work.

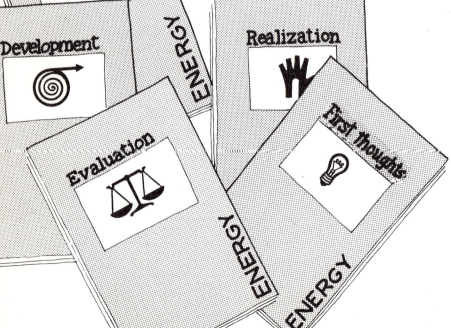

## Organizing the pages

Always leave a margin (about 10mm) all the way round your work. It should not be drawn in, unless it is for a special effect, or you are preparing a final measured workshop drawing.

If possible always work on a standard size of paper – preferably A4 and A3. It should be white and plain – i.e. not lined. It does not matter if you use the paper in the portrait or landscape position, but whichever you choose stick to it all the way through the project.

Try and get into the habit of numbering each page as you work and adding a running title to clarify which aspect of the project you are working on.

Add in special title pages to show where the main sections of research, development and final realization and evaluation come. Finally, prepare a front cover with your name, class or group and date, together with an appropriate illustration.

Make sure you fasten all the pages together in some way.

## Titles

Think carefully about the lettering for titles: don't just put them anywhere and anyhow. Try and choose the height and width of the letters so that the whole title will be well balanced on the page. If the title is too big it may dominate the whole sheet, or if it is too small it might not be noticed.

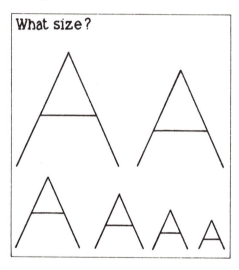

What size?

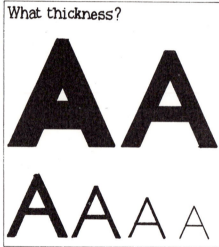

What thickness?

What style?

# Presentation (2)

## Illustrations

Aim to get into the habit of writing and thinking about illustrations at the same time.

Include as many different types of illustrations as possible – maps, plans, elevations, isometrics, axonometrics, perspectives, charts, diagrams, cut-aways, details, etc. Don't forget the possibility of showing what three-dimensional objects are like on the inside as well as the outside.

When adding in photographs, **don't** stick them on with sticky tape, staples or photo mounts. A small amount of paper or card adhesive applied all the way round the edge is the most effective way of fixing them.

## Sketches

Sketches – the drawings you do to help develop your ideas – should be quick and rough. They should **never** be drawn with a ruler, which takes a long time and gives an accuracy usually not necessary at this stage. Don't let your sketches get too rough though – a crude scribble is just a bit too quick.

## Final presentation sheets

Presentations of your final proposals should be very neat. Start by making a list of everything that will need to be included, and decide what would best be described by words, and what by illustrations.

Next, plan the layout of the sheet by drawing a series of small sketches. Then work up the **whole** of the presentation on the final sheet very lightly in pencil, so that if you make any mistakes you can easily erase them.

Try and avoid underlining things or boxing paragraphs and illustrations in. It is better to use space instead, or add emphasis through using different colours.

When everything is right, work the drawing up in a permanent ink line and add colours and textured surfaces. Go over the titles and words in ink too.

Don't forget that this work must be as neat and accurate as it possibly can be. This is when you should be sure to use straight-edge guides and compasses wherever possible. Take great care with colour – use even strokes which exactly fill the space they are meant to, unless a special effect is being applied

*Above: an example of a layout planning sheet (A4 size). Each small rectangle represents a sheet of A3 paper. The wavy lines represent specific pieces of text.*

*Note how the sizes and positions of the title, text and illustrations have been changed around to try and achieve a better visual balance across the page.*

## ASSESSMENT CHECKLIST

Help your teacher to see how much thinking and planning of your presentation you've done by:
- [ ] being careful about how you work on each page
- [ ] providing running titles
- [ ] organizing your preparatory work into a folder at the end of the project
- [ ] using rough, but clear, sketches
- [ ] carefully working out final presentation sheets
- [ ] producing them as neatly as possible.

# Imagination (1)

Designing involves using your imagination to think and feel what different things might be like. How good are you at imagining things? Probably a lot better than you realize. In your mind's eye you are capable of seeing shapes and forms in different colours, hearing all sorts of sounds, and experiencing a whole range of smells, tastes and textures. And even better, you can make the images move and change size, and control the volume and pitch of the sounds ....

**ASSIGNMENT**

Read the following passage very carefully. Concentrate on imagining as vividly as you can the senses which are described. You might find it more effective if you shut your eyes and get someone else to read the passage out to you.

... Imagine yourself on the deck of a large ocean liner, somewhere in the mid Pacific. It is a beautiful day, the sky is clear blue, and the sea quite calm. Feel the heat of the afternoon sun, broken only by a fresh occasional sea breeze. Listen to the gentle swish of the surf and the seagulls calling overhead. Become aware of the gentle vibration of the ship's powerful engines, and the slow but steady movement through the water.

It is a perfect day – everyone is relaxed and carefree. Turn and look up and down the deck, where you can see passengers sunbathing, swimming in the pool, playing deck games, taking tea. Crew members pass by, smartly dressed in clean white uniforms; some are cleaning, others supervising children or serving drinks. Look up to the bridge. See the captain and the helmsman reassuringly steer the ship ever onwards.

Suddenly from somewhere deep down inside the ship comes a strange rumbling sound, and the boat shudders a little. Then, the unbelievable happens. Right in front of you a massive explosion rips apart the back of the ship where the engines are. The noise is deafening, and you find yourself being blown back onto the deck. The heat is scorching and there is soon fire everywhere. Taste the charred smoke, and become aware of the shouts and screams of the passengers and the high-pitched screech of the alarm signals.

Realize that the ship is doomed and you must try and get off – fast. Stagger to your feet. Discover that your leg hurts, and stagger painfully in the direction of a lifeboat that you can see being prepared in front of you. Summon up your final ounce of strength and haul yourself into the last boat.

In your dazed state, sense the rocking of the lifeboat as it begins to drift off. Look out across the water. There is debris everywhere, but everyone seems to have been rescued. Turn and notice the other people in the boat with you.

Time passes. In the distance see the smouldering wreck of your ship sink gracefully and finally into the ocean. Your boat drifts for days. The nights are cold, quiet and dark, except for the wonder of a clear starry night. The days are long, hot and often misty. Then just when you are giving up hope, someone spots a tropical island on the horizon. A few hours later you arrive at the beach. Mentally and physically exhausted you wade from the boat and collapse on the sand ...

You could also now use this passage as the basis for drama work. Work in a group and take the part of one of the crew or passengers, acting out the whole sequence of events.

This time you can add in a lot more detail, and work out what different characters are doing at the time of the explosion, and how they each escape.
- Are you a member of the crew or a passenger?
- What were you wearing?
- Where were you and what were you doing just before the explosion?
- Who were you with?
- How badly injured were you in the explosion?
- Were you able to help anyone to safety?
- Who else ended up in the lifeboat with you?
- How do you feel?
- What do you say to each other?

# Shipwrecked!

Along with other surviving crew and passengers from your ship you find yourself on the beach of a tropical desert island. There appears to be plenty of fruit and vegetables to eat, so none of you will starve. But there are no signs of there ever having been human life.

The island is also teeming with wildlife – sheep, goats, exotic birds and insects. There is nothing larger than a pig, however, and remember that all the animals are wild and have never seen a human being before.

A number of lifeboats and rafts have all ended up together on one island. Some single boats arrived at other distant islands. Decide whether you are part of the larger group, or with one of the smaller parties. Make a clear statement as to how many men, women and children there are.

Before landing you had drifted for many days, and so the island is well away from the main shipping routes. The radio is beyond repair and so there is no means of sending a rescue message. By now search planes will have given up looking, and everyone presumed missing. You might be there for months, even years.

So what is it going to be like trying to survive? What problems will there be? How might they be solved with only the very limited tools and materials which are available?

A few things were rescued in small quantities from the ship and survived the journey. They can be used to help – possibly in different ways than those they were originally intended for. Other survivors may want to use them for different things, so you will always need to make out a very good case to include them in any of your plans.

Information?
Everyday objects?
Transport?
Food and water?
Clothing?
Work, rest and play?
Shelter?
Design and society?
Community?
Fair exchange?

**Map labels:** Raft · Hills and Trees · Lake · Sand · Trees · Cliffs · Sand · Sharks

sack of flour

2 empty oil drums

Odd pieces of assorted metal

polythene sheeting

Coil of rope

A broken radio-receiver

20 biscuit tins (unopened)

20 blankets

10 quilts

5 pairs of assorted old shoes

6 life belts

odd lengths of fabric

20 tins of rice pudding

10 1-litre empty plastic containers

bottle of cooking oil

Tool box with saw, hammer pliers, drill and some nails

can opener

A broken camera

20 balls of thin string

compass

padlock and key

10 papercups

100 drinking straws

assorted safety pins

5 pocket knives

5 pairs of scissors

axe head

small amount of plastic tubing

25 sheets of best quality writing paper

hand mirror

first-aid kit

**THE JU-JU POD** — Mark Jennings

Going Further......

## To Be rescued — Page 3

1. Smoke signals - do from top of highest hill - the one on N E of Island with plateau (see map). Clear a bit of forest with axe head tied to stick. Build a fire with wood cleared and light with either strips of material or paper. It can be lit with suns rays deflected off a hand mirror and onto paper. To stop smoke and cause a 'signal' than a 'blanket' part of a torn up quilt could be used.

Morse Code SOS - fires could be lit at night with the flint-sparks on 2 sticks together techniques.

**SMOKE SIGNALS.**

Messages to be signalled:
SOS.
please give us a radio!
get us out of here.!

## COMMUNII — Original 'idea(s)'....... Page 5

(as opposed to conventional)

WARNING!
This idea is not likely to work very well and is not very effective anyway!.

in cons (rice pudding) strewn across trees with in string, this would warn the camp of attacking 'big animals or when to attack them (for their din-dins).

Boring ideas such as:
Banging drums, stones down cliffs, etc. These all could be used but do not need to be described in detail.
And a last resort (only to be used once).

What we need:
Ship on the horizon.
oil drums
cooking oil
and everything else
lightable.
newspaper
logs.

What we do:
make a bonfire,
light it with mirror,
run!.

Conclusion:
The island will soon be a ball of flame, easily sighted by passing ships
(you ideas have to swim until help arrives

# Survival (2)

Don't forget to bear in mind the limitations of the tools and materials which are available to you. Also remember to consider that some of the people who you are shipwrecked with may be very young or old, or have other special needs you will have to take into consideration.

Working individually or in groups, choose one or several of the following topic headings. Prepare illustrated A3 sheets and models to present in detail your ideas in response to the starting questions which are posed. You can also tackle any other problems which occur to you.

*Speech bubbles: How long would it take to make? How would it be made? What would it look like? Why is it needed? What size would it be? What is it made from? What does it do? How does it do it? Where would it be kept? Would it be safe?*

## Clothing

The clothes you were wearing when your ship went down are now ripped, shrunk and hanging off. Modesty, and the tropical climate, mean that you need some new garments to protect you from the burning sun, the dampness of the forests and rivers, and the cold of the night. They will have to be fairly simple and quick to make from the resources you have, and at the same time easy to get into and move about in.

Investigate the potential of natural sources of dyes – fruits, vegetables, etc. Collect as many as you can and conduct a series of experiments to see which are the most effective.

How could patterns be made? Explore basic methods such as finger-painting and block printing using natural objects.

• Wash your hands!
• Not to be eaten!

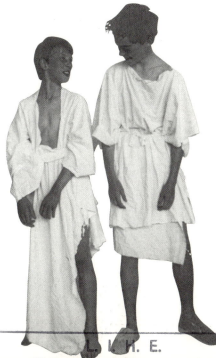

L. I. H. E.

- What sort of footwear will you need, and why?
- Why might a hat of some sort be needed?
- How can fabrics be dyed and decorated?
- Can the garments be washed?
- How could you spin wool?
- How could you knit or weave?

## Design and society

What ideas have you got to improve the general quality of life for all on the island?

What measures need to be taken in order to preserve the natural resources of the island?

What special materials, tools and systems will be needed to deal with the following situations?

- What rules should there be? How will law and order be most effectively maintained?
- Should there be leaders? How will they be chosen?
- Should there be any formal learning and education? Who would it be provided for, and how?
- Should any religious ceremonies be held? How will morale be kept high?

continued ...

# Survival (3)

## Food and water

Luckily there was a small supply of emergency rations in your lifeboat which have kept you all alive so far, but are just about to run out. One of your first priorities therefore will need to be to find some food and water. After a few days of fending for yourselves you realize that things need to be more organized.

- How can spring and rain water be collected and stored?
- How can water be carried to where it is needed?
- What plans can be made in case of drought?

- How long can the different types of food be stored for?
- Where should it be stored?
- How should it be rationed?
- How can you catch small animals, or fish?

- How are you going to prepare the food?
- What needs to be cooked, and how will you do it without burning the food?
- What other utensils will you need to cook and eat with?
- In the long term what will you need to eat to ensure your diet is balanced?

## Transport

There is often a need to carry fruit and vegetables in bulk, and to move heavy logs and rocks to difficult parts of the island. How could this be made easier? Remember there are no roads!

What other transportation devices might be needed? How could they be made?

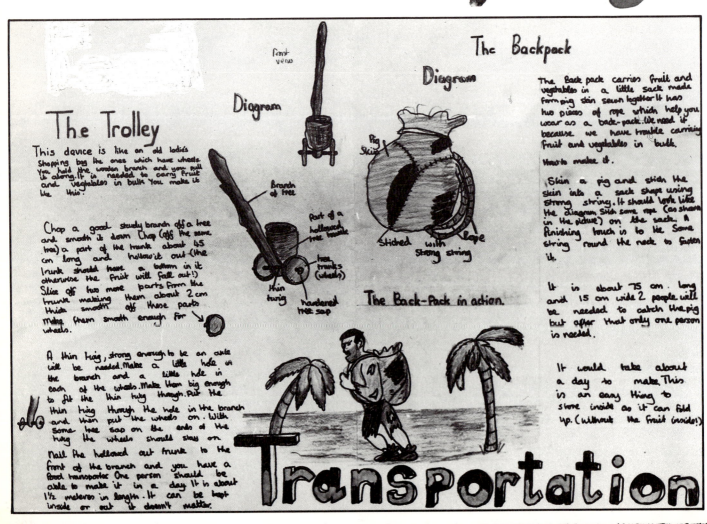

## Work, rest and play

Make a list of the everyday tasks which will need to be undertaken.

Which could be done more effectively by a group of people (e.g. preparing food, building houses, etc.)?

Should men and women do different jobs?

At the end of a hard day's work how will everyone relax and entertain themselves?

Design something comfortable to sleep on.

Unfortunately there is no record player, or any books on the island. Pass away some of the long hours explaining which eight gramophone records you would like to have been cast away with and why, and which books you would have chosen. What would your luxury item have been?

Write and illustrate a story, short enough to be remembered and told, about an imaginary incident which has happened on the island. Base your idea on an ancient myth, substituting the island and its inhabitants.

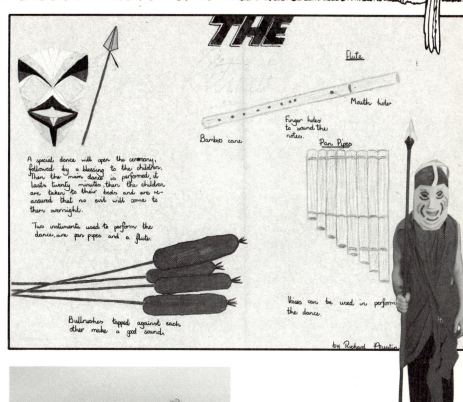

A special dance will open the ceremony, followed by a blessing to the children. Then the main dance is performed, it lasts twenty minutes, then the children are taken to their beds and are re-assured that no evil will come to them overnight.

Two instruments used to perform the dance, are pan pipes and a flute.

Bullrushes tapped against each other make a good sound.

*Flute*
*Bamboo cane*
*Mouth hole*
*Finger holes to sound the notes.*
*Pan Pipes*
*Voices can be used in perform the dance.*

by Richard Austin

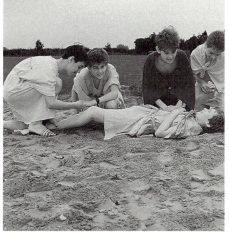

It is someone's birthday. Remembering the limitations of what is available, plan a simple party for them, based on a particular theme. Devise some simple games which involve the unusual use of things found on the island. Present your idea by writing and illustrating a diary record of what happened.

Design and make a simple toy for a young child who has been shipwrecked with you.

Design and make some devices to make musical sounds when struck, blown or vibrated. Devise a musical notation for each instrument, and write down a simple group composition.

Several younger children are frightened by the noises and darkness of the night. Devise a ritual to perform an imaginary magical function which will reassure them. Design and make masks and costumes, and work out the sequence of actions.

Costumes for play to reassure children

The Goody    The Baddy

masks! →

Died palm leaves

Diary Day 13

Today we decided to build a totem-pole as a record of our stay on the island. We discussed what images we should carve into it and where it should be placed.

Tonight is my turn to guard the camp. Last night to help keep myself amused I started to make a chess-board and some pieces.

I am starting to enjoy being here now.

*continued...*

# Survival (5)

## Shelter

Some form of shelter will also be an important priority. Something will be needed to provide protection from wild animals at night, to store and keep things safely, and to afford some privacy.

There are several different possible approaches to building a simple shelter, involving different constructional methods and materials. Undertake some small-scale experiments. When you have found what you think is the best method, consider the following:

- What interior spaces will be needed?
- How big should they be?

## Community

- How will a number of shelters be grouped together?
- What communal structures might be required?
- Will any boundaries and fences be necessary?
- What will the settlement be called?

## Fair exchange

Naturally there are no banks on the island, and credit cards won't get you very far either. Somehow though, people will probably need some sort of encouragement or persuasion to undertake unpleasant tasks. Is some form of monetary system needed?

- Do the natural resources which are discovered become the property of the person who found them?
- Who do the items found on the beach belong to?
- Does anyone own the tools, clothes and so on which are made there?
- Are there any ways of persuading the animals on the island to perform useful tasks?

## Information

Very occasionally ships can be sighted on the distant horizon, and planes fly high above. If a ship or plane ever came closer, what means could be used to send an SOS message?

Paper and materials are severely limited. As various groups explore the island they need to record and mark where they have been and what they found for future reference. Devise a set of simple signs and symbols, and an easy way they can be marked out.

Think of some other occasions when modern communication devices might have been useful – telling the time, for example, or signalling across the island. What alternative solutions can you come up with?

## Everyday objects

We have come to rely on countless objects which extend our capabilities to perform simple tasks.

- What tools and utensils will be most needed on the island?
- How might they be made?
- Should they be decorated in any way?
- Where will they be kept?

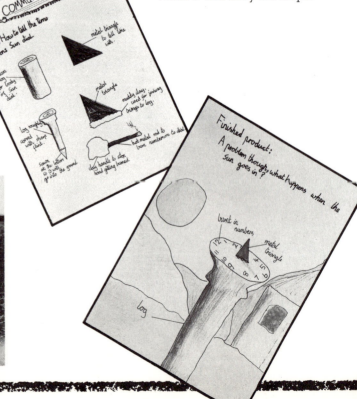

# Rescue

A year has passed. Most of your plans and ideas have worked well and you are still all alive and healthy. Suddenly one day a ship is sighted on the horizon: someone rushes to light a beacon, and before long the ship can be seen steaming towards the island.

How do you feel? Will you be glad to get back home, or are you tempted to stay? What would you miss most about living on the island? What are you especially keen to return to?

A vote is taken, and the majority clearly want to return home.

## Media event

After a long journey you arrive home, and the press are there in force to meet you. Divide into two groups and agree first on a list of questions that as journalists you would want to ask – remember you need a good story with plenty of human interest. Then work out a number of stories which, as shipwrecked islanders, you would like to tell.

Act out a press conference scene, and then reverse your roles. As a newspaper reporter, prepare a front-page story, based on the answers you were given at the press conference.

## Exhibition

Most of the things which were made on the island were brought back as well. The curator of a local museum invites you to prepare a display which will make a lively presentation of the experiences of the shipwrecked islanders.

Work in a group to co-ordinate the exhibition which will include all the models, explanatory sheets and diary accounts which were completed. See if you can find a suitable location in your school to mount the display.

# Everyday products, places & communications

Everything around you which is not completely natural has been designed by someone – usually professional specialist designers. It is possible to identify three broad areas of things which have been designed – **products, places** and **communications**.

**Products** are three-dimensional objects. Some are very small – a piece of jewellery, or a paperclip, for example, whilst others might be very large, such as those which provide transport – aeroplanes, trains and so on. Somewhere between these two extremes come things like cars, clothing, furniture, domestic utensils, machine tools and so on. And food which has been processed in any way would come under this heading too.

**Places**, and spaces, occur when a number of products are brought together. Sometimes they will be in a specially designed structure – a workshop or classroom in a school, for example, or a kitchen in a house. Alternatively they can be outside, such as a park, or a shopping centre. Towns and cities are examples of places which have been designed, too. Architects and planners are usually concerned with these areas.

**Communications** are usually two-dimensional images which exist to pass on or record information, such as advertisements, films and television programmes, record and book covers, newspapers, etc. Graphic designers contribute a great deal to this category. Look through old magazines and collect as wide a variety as possible of different **products, places** and **communications**. Add drawings of your own and produce a collage.

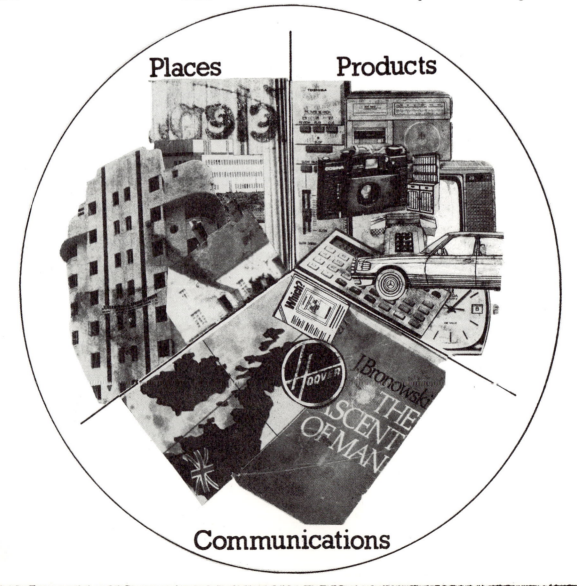

Make a list of all the **places** around your home. Use the names you and your family use – the living room, the spare room, etc. Include passage ways and any large cupboards which form the structure of the house. You can also list all the outdoor places within your garden.

Carefully choose six of the places you have identified and this time make lists of at least six different specific **products** which you could find at home in each of the places.

Then add to your lists at least three different examples of **communications** from each place.

Select three products and one example of communications from each place. At home, go round and find each item and prepare a simple rough sketch of it, noting the colours as well.

In rough, work out a diagram like the one shown – there should be a central circle labelled 'My house', and six satellite circles with the names of the places you chose.

Around each of them should be a further series of four circles, filled with illustrations of details of the items – just enough to make out what each is.

It is important to draw out everything very lightly in pencil first to ensure that all the circles fit reasonably evenly across the page, and that there are no large gaps. Then draw up the final very neat version using a mixture of coloured pencils and felt pens, and black ink lines.

Make sure you keep both your lists and your diagram, as you will find them a useful reference for several other assignments later in the book.

# Community

Although people need private and personal spaces – somewhere to live that they can call their own – they also like to feel part of a group. A really successful community enables a person to remain an individual, whilst also supporting and being helped by other members of the neighbourhood.

At one extreme the whole world, or each continent, is a community. At the other end of the scale your street and house are both communities. No two communities will ever be exactly the same.

Most places have a lot of things in common – roads, buildings, etc., but each village, town, city and country is different. We tell them apart by their

- physical differences, such as location, size and layout
- different characters – what the places feel like when you're in them.

Here are some words commonly used to describe what places feel like:

    cramped, isolated, busy, neglected, lively, boring, quaint, bleak, desolate, charming, historic, pretty, picturesque, barren, friendly.

Use a dictionary to look up any words you don't know the meaning of.

Draw out and complete a chart like the one on the right based on the place you live in.

Choose a different place that you have visited and stayed in and draw up a comparative chart.

| PLACE | | FEATURES |
|---|---|---|
| COUNTY | Kent | Pretty |
| TOWN /CITY | Canterbury | Historic |
| DISTRICT | Northgate | Busy |
| ROAD | Plumpton Walk | Cramped |
| NUMBER | 5 | Modern |

## DISCUSSION ISSUES

In a small group consider the following questions:

- What is it that makes your village, town or city different?
- What is unusual about each of your neighbourhoods?
- What is special about the street you each live in?
- What makes each of your houses or flats stand out from all the others?

Prepare a number of short group statements which sum up your discussion.

# Environmental evaluation

Choose a public space near your school or home. A good site might be your local High Street or shopping centre – somewhere you visit often and know well.

Start by describing the place using sketches, plans and maybe photographs. Then think about its good and bad points – the things you like most and least about the place, and why. Present your findings as a report, or a series of display panels.

Don't forget to try and use some of the 'Evaluation' words from page 8.

## Describing the place
- Where is it and what area does it cover?
- What routes are there for people and transport to move around, and in and out?
- What styles of buildings are there, and what are they used for?
- How are the buildings and public areas grouped together?
- How are public and private areas separated?

## Evaluating the place ⚖
- Is there a sense of community?
- Within the space you have chosen, try and identify any areas in which you feel happy, sad. afraid, relaxed, crowded, alone, etc.
- How easily could strangers find their way round?
- Can you identify any planning faults?

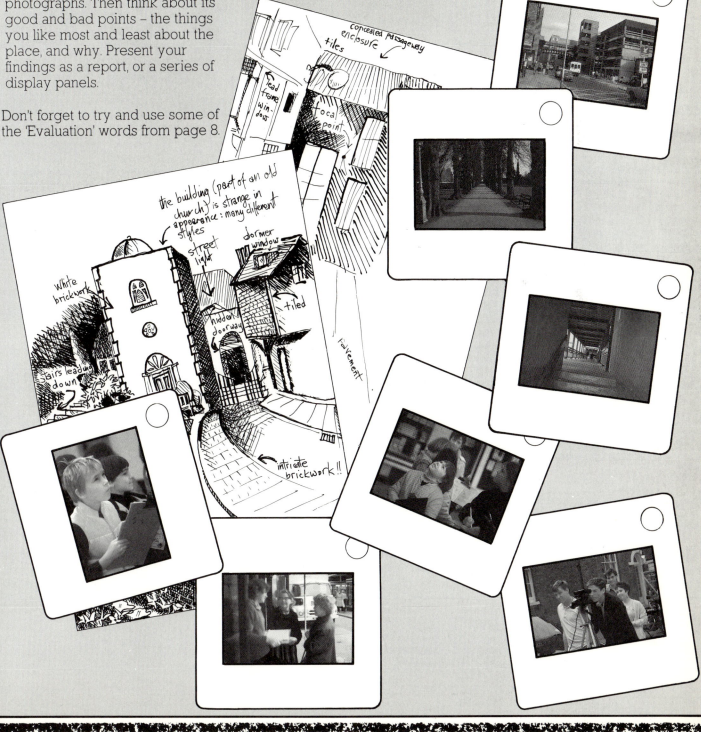

# Schoolscapes (1)

Your school is a small-scale community in which different people come together to undertake a wide variety of activities all concerned with education. There need to be many different sorts of spaces and places to enable everyone to be able to work effectively.

Make a list of all the different people who work at, or often visit, your school. Note down the various spaces and places each needs to use.

## ASSIGNMENTS

### Schoolscape site study

Make a study of the way in which your school grounds are used. The questions on the opposite page should give you some good starting points, but you may be able to think of some other things to consider. Don't forget to use lots of sketches and diagrams to help you record what you discover.

What changes and improvements could you make to the following:
- special play equipment?
- general layout?
- pathways?
- sheds, greenhouses, etc.?
- tidiness?

Present your findings either as an illustrated booklet or a series of A3 display panels. Include a section in which you make suggestions for ways in which the grounds could be improved. A model might be a useful way of presenting your proposals for change.

### Schoolscape event

Working in groups plan a special event to take place once a year in your school grounds. Choose some important aspect of school life as a central theme – the first or last day of term, harvest festival, and so on. Design special posters, banners, flags and costumes and work out songs, music, drama, and dances to perform.
- How much would it cost to make it all happen?
- How could you raise the money?

### Schoolscape sculpture

Find an area of your school grounds you really like or dislike. Produce a piece of two-dimensional art work which expresses your feelings about that particular place. Then design and make a model of a piece of three-dimensional sculpture which could be appropriately placed there.

# Schoolscapes (2)

- How old are the grounds?
- What were they like in the past?
- Can you remember any incidents, ceremonies, special events or other things which have happened in your school grounds?

- What is the main entrance to your school grounds like – inviting and friendly or forbidding and frightening?
- How do people know it is the entrance?
- What other ways in are there?
- What kinds of signs are used to give information?

- What wildlife and animals are there in your school grounds?
- Do they live there or just visit?
- What different sorts of trees, plants and flowers grow there?
- How many different ways are the trees used?
- Do they form screens or boundaries?

- Which trees have special names as places to meet or go to?
- Where do paths go to and from?
- What are they made of?
- What condition are they in?
- Are they in the right place?
- What short-cuts do people take?

- How do you feel about the different areas of your school grounds?
- Where is your favourite place to go and sit outside?
- What makes it so attractive?
- Which parts do you avoid going to?
- Why do you dislike being there?
- Do other people feel the same way?

- What games do you like to play in the school grounds?
- Which places do you go to play them?
- Which ones can only be played in certain places?
- Are there any items of special play equipment, like swings, climbing frames and so on?
- Which are your favourite outdoor games?

- What kinds of spaces are there in the school grounds?
- What size and shape are they?
- Who uses them?
- How many people use them at one time, and at different times?
- Are any spaces used for more than one purpose?

- How are the spaces enclosed or divided up?
- Are the grounds flat or of varying levels?
- What is the surrounding area of the school like?
- Looking out from the grounds what can you see?

# City centre community

Find out what you can about the planning ideas behind these four examples.

*The Garden City Movement of the turn of this century*

*A Greek or Roman city*

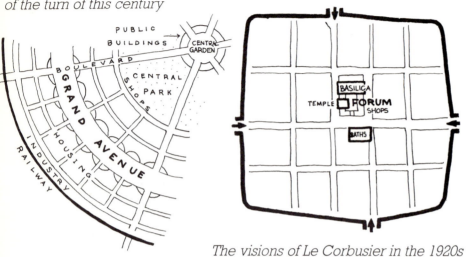

*The visions of Le Corbusier in the 1920s*

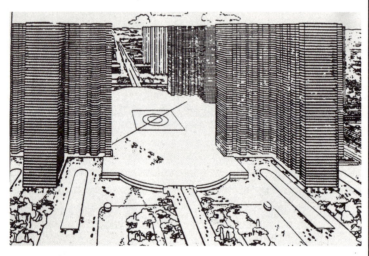

*Milton Keynes in the 1970s and 1980s*

Towns and cities don't just happen: they are planned and designed to be the way they are. A city is more than just a layout of buildings, paths and roadways: there are many things which are needed to make towns and cities successful communities to live and work in, such as:

- public as well as private space
- a transportation system which enables people to move around easily and cheaply
- housing which is suitable for people of differing incomes, ages and family groupings
- adequate leisure and recreation facilities
- a variety of types of shops
- provision for industry and commerce (factories and offices)
- access to schools, hospitals and other services
- an effective city centre.

Prepare a short illustrated report about the possible future growth and change of the nearest town or city to where you live.

Use the headings above to help structure your report. You could concentrate on just one, or cover several points in varying detail. Describe:

- the things which concern you or other members of the public at present
- how and why these problems could get worse in the next ten years
- why they are important issues
- ways in which the situation could be improved.

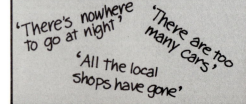

'There's nowhere to go at night'

'There are too many cars'

'All the local shops have gone'

# Local issues

Identify a real site in your nearest town or city which is vacant, or due for redevelopment. Make a simple proposal for the way in which it should come to be used – a new shopping centre perhaps, or a car park, sports centre, etc.

Imagine you are:
● a local trader
● an old age pensioner
● a parent with three young children
● a policeman
● any other appropriate character
and consider how each might react to the proposals. What advantages and disadvantages might each see?

Prepare a series of 'role-play' cards, and improvise a planning enquiry meeting. You will need a chairperson to keep order! At the end take a vote to see if the proposal is accepted or rejected by the majority.

# Planning your own city

This activity could be undertaken individually, in small groups, or as described here, as a class project.

You have been asked to submit outline planning proposals for an imaginary new city near the Channel Tunnel in south east Kent.

Make lists of the things your community will need and want (like low-cost housing and large park areas) and all the things they won't want (like large estates and pollution).

Draw a series of sketch diagrams to establish some possible overall layouts for the city.

When you have agreed on the best approach, allocate each member of the group a responsibility for developing certain areas of the plan – shopping, transport interchange, civic centre, and so on. Keep discussing your proposals with others in your group to check that your ideas are not conflicting with those of other people.

Draw up final plan layouts to as large a scale as possible.

Think up a suitable name for your city.

# Everyday objects (1)

This section is concerned with everyday things which have already been designed by someone else. We take most of them for granted, but someone somewhere has spent a great deal of time and effort working out what size, shape and colour everything should be, what it will do, how it will do it, and how it is going to be made.

As we discovered on page 6, we are surrounded by **products** – three-dimensional everyday objects which serve us in a wide variety of different ways.

It is possible to identify all these products as either **extenders** or **containers**. Extenders exist to improve our ability to perform particular tasks – scissors, bicycles and musical instruments are obvious examples. Containers make our lives more comfortable and simple – clothing, packaging, chairs and so on. Of course some items are both containers and extenders, like motor cars.

The very first everyday objects to be designed were probably arrowheads and simple knives, crudely shaped from pieces of stone. Even these, however, had to follow the basic requirements for successful design, because they had to:

- be simple, comfortable and convenient to use
- work effectively
- be relatively easy to manufacture
- last as long as possible.

Many early spears, farming implements, pots and so on were also often elaborately decorated, revealing another important design requirement – that the object had to

- be pleasing to look at.

During the Industrial Revolution, however, engineers and factory owners often concentrated on how things worked and could be made as cheaply as possible. They rarely thought about how objects might be designed and made to be more comfortable, easier to use, or how they looked.

It was only after World War II that everyday objects started to be designed more from the point of view of the person who would end up using them. It was recognized that humans have certain physical abilities and limitations – how far they can reach, or bend, for example. These are known as **ergonomic** considerations.

Victorian gas lamp

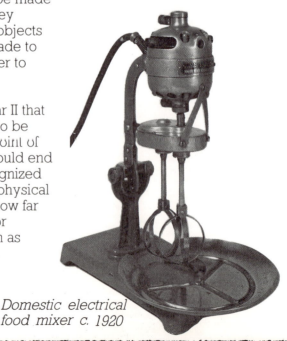

Domestic electrical food mixer c. 1920

# Everyday objects (2)

Complex control panels and displays in cars, aeroplanes and on computer keyboards, are now organized to be as easy as possible for the operator to see, understand and use. And even things such as cutlery and toothbrushes are now designed with the capabilities of the user in mind.

The visual qualities of objects are also now given a higher priority. If two cars, two cookers or two computers perform in roughly the same way and cost about the same, then the way they look will often be the deciding influence in choosing which to buy. And although people rarely admit it, being seen to be fashionable is not the last, but often the first consideration.

## Human factors

Working in a group of about six, chose an everyday household object, such as a telephone, a microwave oven, etc. and construct it using the materials provided – which are yourselves!

Think carefully about the operations and movements involved, and don't forget to add appropriate sounds. Can others in your class identify the object?

Imagine **you** are one of the everyday objects you have at home. Draw a picture of yourself, as the object and add cartoon 'bubbles' which contain some of your thoughts and feelings about the life you lead.

- How old are you?
- Are you in good health?
- Do you like your work?
- What do you think of your owner?
- Have you had any interesting experiences?

# Product evaluation

Carefully choose a three-dimensional everyday object. Your task is first to describe it in detail using a mixture of words and pictures, and then to report on how well you think it has been designed.

When you evaluate the object you may have to undertake some tests to discover how well it works. Other comments will need to be your own opinions. After you have presented your own conclusions, find out if other people agree with them or not.

## Describing the object
- What is it supposed to do?
- How does it do it?
- What is it made from?
- How is it put together?
- What does it look and feel like?

## Evaluating the object
- How well does it work?
- Is it easy to use?
- Is it well made?
- Is it repairable?
- Do you like the way it looks and feels?
- Is it good value for money?

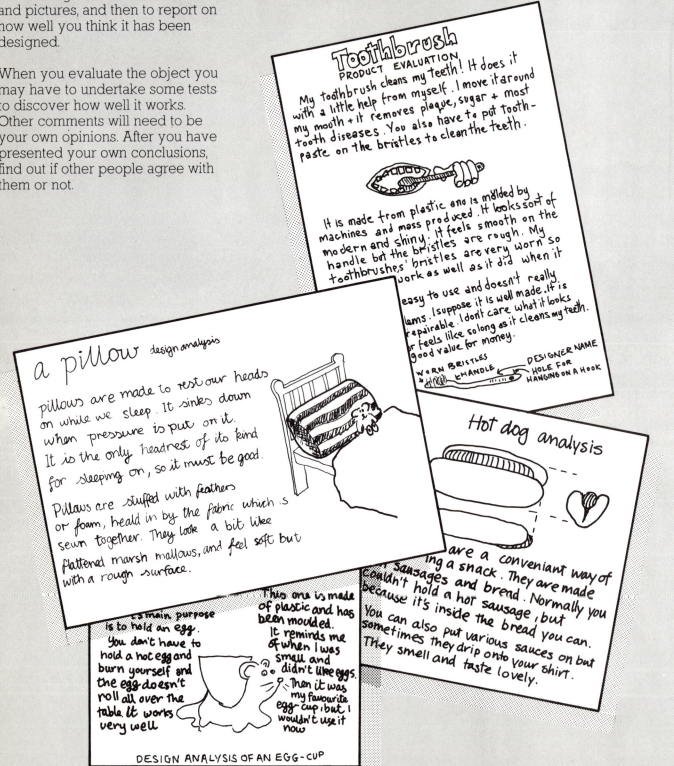

### Toothbrush
PRODUCT EVALUATION

My toothbrush cleans my teeth! It does it with a little help from myself. I move it around my mouth + it removes plaque, sugar + most tooth diseases. You also have to put tooth-paste on the bristles to clean the teeth.

It is made from plastic and is molded by machines and mass produced. It looks sort of modern and shiny. It feels smooth on the handle but the bristles are rough. My toothbrushes' bristles are very worn so work as well as it did when it

easy to use and doesn't really lems. I suppose it is well made. It is repairable. I don't care what it looks r feels like so long as it cleans my teeth. good value for money.

WORN BRISTLES
HANDLE
DESIGNER NAME
HOLE FOR HANGING ON A HOOK

### a pillow design analysis

Pillows are made to rest our heads on while we sleep. It sinks down when pressure is put on it. It is the only headrest of its kind for sleeping on, so it must be good.

Pillows are stuffed with feathers or foam, held in by the fabric which is sewn together. They look a bit like flattened marsh mallows, and feel soft but with a rough surface.

### Hot dog analysis

are a conveniant way of ing a snack. They are made sausages and bread. Normally you couldn't hold a hot sausage, but because it's inside the bread you can. You can also put various sauces on but sometimes they drip onto your shirt They smell and taste lovely.

s main purpose is to hold an egg.
You don't have to hold a hot egg and burn yourself and the egg doesn't roll all over the table. It works very well

This one is made of plastic and has been moulded. It reminds me of when I was small and didn't like eggs. Then it was my favourite egg cup but I wouldn't use it now

DESIGN ANALYSIS OF AN EGG-CUP

# Nice and nasty (1)

Some sensations need only be put into words for us to be able to feel them in our imaginations. A musician uses sounds and rhythms to express feelings and moods, and an artist presents us with a composition of colours, tones and shapes – a brilliant warm red can create a different feeling to a dull murky green, and a circle gives a different feeling to a sharply pointed triangular form.

Without realizing it we often react in a similar way to **everyday objects**. The colours, shapes and textures of a well designed product can make us feel reassured, excited, comforted and so on, whilst others produce feelings of unease or tension. Sometimes it is because we are reminded of past pleasant or unpleasant events.

## MAJOR ASSIGNMENT

Select six different objects found around your home or at school. Produce a coloured and textured drawing of each and say in words how each of them makes you feel.

Find out how to make a polyhedral (many-sided) shape with between six and ten sides – or make a box that has a similar number of sections or compartments.

Make a list of contrasting nice and nasty emotional words, such as rage and excitement, fear and comfort, happiness and pain, etc. Use a combination of a range of scrap materials and small everyday objects to try and express those feelings. Fix each representation to a side of the polyhedral shape you have made, or place it into the compartment of your box.

Test your ideas by asking others in your group if they can work out what feelings you were trying to communicate.

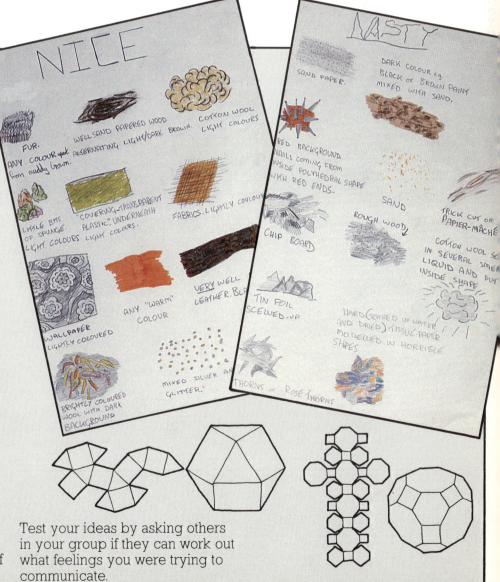

*continued ...*

# Nice and nasty (2)

Diary
I decided to use nice lush green vegetation to suggest something living, and in contrast, something which was all dead and burnt. On another of the 'Nice' surfaces I used bright colours to glitter and be strong and to appear to come out of the shape, so that if people see it they're more likely to go towards it to see what it's actually like.

# Everyday objectivity

We rarely buy the first thing we see. It is always wise to find out which brand has the features we need, looks and feels the way we want it to, and provides the best overall value for our money.

Working in small groups make a small collection of everyday pencils and assorted pens. Check you will be able to identify which are yours at the end of the session.

Write the name, manufacturer and model number down if you can, or make up your own description to identify it.

Identify the main product types – e.g. pencils, fibre-tip pens, OHP markers, etc., and draw up onto a chart a full-size elevation of the writing end. Add a sample of the type of line it actually produces.

At the bottom of the chart try and identify what type of work each pen is most suited to – sketching, writing, etc – on certain surfaces.

Choose one of the groups of product types you have identified and devise a series of controlled tests to compare each pen or pencil.
- How long does it last?
- Does it dry up quickly if the cap is left off?
- Is the cap easy to put on and take off?
- Does it look good?
- How much does it cost?

Draw up an illustrated chart to show what you discover. Which pens give the best value for money? How reliable and accurate do you think your tests were? How could they be improved?

What tests could you undertake to discover how well the following worked?
- a packet of crisps
- a paper towel
- a novelty pencil sharpener
- some other everyday object

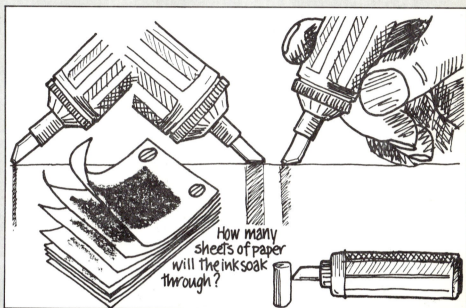

How many sheets of paper will the ink soak through?

The lead in 'd' seemed to break more often

'b' had the best pattern printed on it

Because 'c' is round it kept rolling away

so which would you buy?

How long before sharpening?

cost per dozen

# A museum of design

Most people's homes are full of everyday objects which were first acquired at some time during this century. Many items may only have been purchased very recently, but others may have originally been used by grandparents or other relatives, and handed on when your parents set up house. Some things just seem to survive longer than others.

Certain objects may be even older and have become valuable antiques, but this assignment is about ordinary everyday objects which may well still be in use.

**ASSIGNMENT**

Ask your parents or relatives which objects in your home have survived the longest (not counting any antiques).

- How old are they?
- Where did they come from?
- How much did they cost?
- How did they work?
- How useful were they?
- What are they used for now?
- In what ways are present-day designs different or similar?

Make sketches and coloured drawings of the object, and ask if you can borrow it to take into school. As a group mount a temporary display of your everyday objects with written descriptions of the history of each item.

'My dad got this tie in Carnaby Street in 1967'

'My uncle gave me this ticket from the Festival of Britain Exhibition of 1951'

'These are coasters from the 1920's. My grandma bought them for 6d in a local junk shop'

'In the early 1950s we didn't have many electrical appliances. When I did the ironing I used my parents' flatiron which they had received as a wedding present in 1912. It was made of iron, black in colour and very heavy.

I had to heat it up on the gas stove and try to judge exactly the right heat to iron various fabrics without scorching, and a very tricky job it was. Of course I had to have two irons on the go – one heating up as the other was being used. I always had to remember to pick it up using a special square of cloth so that I didn't burn my hands.

One day my iron was too hot and unfortunately I burnt a hole in my little boy's shorts! Eventually we purchased a steam iron which was absolutely wonderful because it was lighter, thermostatically controlled, and much easier to use – I could just set the dial to the type of fabric to be ironed.

I still have my flatirons, however, only now they are used as doorstops!'

# Fantastic inventions

A hundred years ago few people would have believed it would ever be possible to see and hear something else going on on the other side of the world, or that someone could ever fly to the moon.

Imagine you were suddenly transported back into a different century and found yourself trying to describe and explain what some of today's designs and inventions were like.

... and it's called a camera

*Mechanical feeder foreseen for 1985 in 1885*

Choose one of the following, and prepare some notes about how it works and what it does. Without naming the object, read your explanations out and see if the others in your group can work out what you have been describing.

- an egg whisk
- a compact disc player
- a credit card
- a solar-powered calculator
- a zip fastener
- some other everyday item

## Not-so-fantastic inventions?

If you were then suddenly transported one hundred years into the future, what do you think might have been invented that is hard for us to believe today? Make a list of some inventions which you think would be very useful, even if they seem quite impossible at present. Make similar lists for different people you know.

Some possible starting points are:
- safety
- exploration
- doing things more quickly
- communication
- getting rid of unpleasant jobs.

Choose one of your inventions and prepare a drawing and written description of it, saying what it does, why it would be useful, and how parts of it might be made.

If possible make a three-dimensional (non-working!) model of it, using card, scrap wood, modelling clay, pieces of fabric or any other appropriate materials.

State how likely you think it is that your invention could exist in the future. What are the biggest problems yet to be solved? Can you think of any potential disadvantages in such an invention?

*Submarine water bus*

# Hidden uses (1)

We use the everyday things which surround us in many different ways.

For example, the main purpose of a dining chair is to sit on whilst eating at a table. We call this its **primary function**.

But a dining chair can also be used for other things too – like standing on in order to change a light bulb, or maybe even as protection for a lion tamer! These sorts of other uses are known as **secondary functions**. What other uses can you think of for a dining chair?

'We bought this lovely set of dining chairs while we were on holiday in France

The man in the shop said that they were once owned by Louis the 16th'

'This is the high-chair my father made for me.

I couldn't bear to throw it out'

'When people see me sitting in the biggest chair, it reminds them that I am in charge here'

There is also a third way in which we use everyday objects, concerned not so much with their physical or practical uses, but with the things we think about them – how they make us feel. These can be described as **tertiary functions**.

Tertiary functions often involve our memories of how things used to be, or enable us to say things in a very subtle way about the sort of person we are, or would perhaps like to be.

Maybe your dining chair was once owned by someone famous, or made especially for you by a favourite relative. Or it might be that it is very rare, valuable, part of a collection, or particularly pleasing to look at – all things which would serve to remind you and your friends how knowledgeable and wealthy you are, and what good taste you have.

Whenever something is being designed it is important to consider the possible **secondary** and **tertiary** uses it might have, as well as its **primary** function.

# Hidden uses (2)

Make lists of as many different **primary, secondary** and **tertiary** functions as you can for:

- a teaspoon
- a child's building brick
- a book
- a paperclip.

Refer back to your list of **products** found around your home (see page 27). Choose three different items and list their **primary, secondary** and **tertiary** uses. If you find an item you have chosen difficult to do, leave it and try another.

Select the item for which you have the best range of **secondary** and **tertiary** uses, and prepare in rough some cartoons to illustrate each of your ideas.

When you have worked your ideas out, draw up a neat A3 presentation sheet along the lines of the ones reproduced below. Don't forget to add colour and texture to the drawings. Pay special attention to the spacing between the drawings and the captions, and make sure you achieve a visual balance across the sheet.

How big or small will each illustration need to be?

What titles and captions will be needed to explain the ideas?

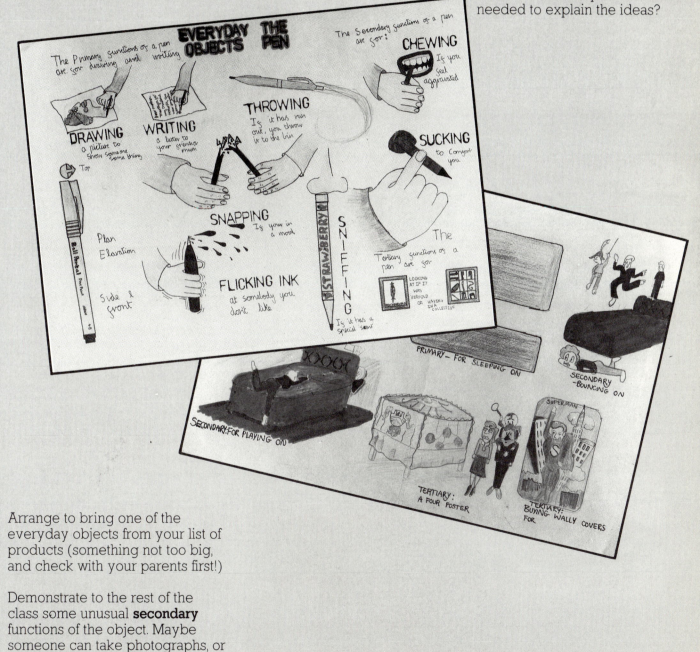

Arrange to bring one of the everyday objects from your list of products (something not too big, and check with your parents first!)

Demonstrate to the rest of the class some unusual **secondary** functions of the object. Maybe someone can take photographs, or record you performing on video tape?

# Fair exchange

How do we set about satisfying our basic needs for food, shelter, warmth, etc.? If we are hungry, for example, there are four possibilities. The first is to go out hunting, fishing or gathering fruit for ourselves. The second way is to steal food from someone else, and a third is to beg from someone else who already has enough. But today none of these options are particularly convenient, or socially acceptable.

Luckily there is the fourth option – you can offer to **exchange** something of your own with someone else who has more food than they need. You may be able to offer some item or useful service in return or, more likely, an agreed sum of money.

This is the concept on which our whole way of life is now based. By being able to provide specialized goods or services we are able to exchange them for food, clothing, shelter and all the other things we need to survive. And depending how much our own goods and services are in demand, we might end up with more than we essentially **need**, and be able to obtain some of the things we just **want**.

To make such exchanges easier we have set up **markets** – circumstances in which people can present the goods and services they have to offer, and other people can decide if they wish to purchase them or not.

We are all familiar with street markets, but shops, showrooms, mail-order catalogues and classified newspaper advertisements are also all examples of different sorts of markets.

You may also have heard of the term **marketing**, which put simply, is the professional business of finding out

- what people need and want
- how much money they are willing to exchange for those goods and services
- the most suitable type of market to present and offer particular goods in
- the most effective way of informing people of the availability and desirability of what is being offered for exchange.

So marketing involves a great deal more than just asking people to fill in questionnaires or designing clever advertisements to sell people things they don't really want. Most major business organizations invest a great deal of time and money in marketing in order to be as sure as possible that their investments in providing new products and services will not be wasted.

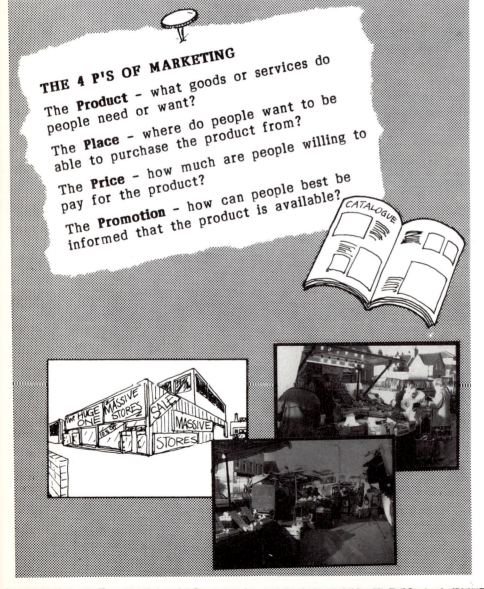

THE 4 P'S OF MARKETING

The **Product** – what goods or services do people need or want?

The **Place** – where do people want to be able to purchase the product from?

The **Price** – how much are people willing to pay for the product?

The **Promotion** – how can people best be informed that the product is available?

# Commercial break (1)

## Selling dreams

It's not much use having goods or services to exchange or sell if no one knows about them or wants to buy them. Most businesses need to **promote** the products they have, and suggest to us that our life will be more comfortable and enjoyable if we possess them.

If only a few people buy a particular item, the manufacturing company might go out of business and make its workforce redundant. But when a product sells in large quantities, it can be made and sold more cheaply. This in turn provides employment, not just for the company workers, but for haulage firms, shop keepers and so on.

Advertising is therefore used to inform us of the goods and services a company has made available, and what they might do for us. The first advertisements used for commercial purposes can be traced back to ancient Greece, but it was not until the end of the Industrial Revolution in the last century that advertising really established itself. In those days advertisements were fairly simple, and generally stuck to the facts.

In the past twenty years, however, advertisements have become a great deal more sophisticated and clever. Sometimes they persuade us to buy things we perhaps think we want, but don't really need. Understandably they never present the disadvantages of the product (e.g. sweets can ruin our teeth and make us fat!). And modern advertisements also often have the effect of making us feel more generally dissatisfied with life. Very few people are ever able to afford the high-performance cars, the dream homes and the exotic holidays which we see day after day in magazines and on television.

Of course advertisements are not allowed to make false claims about the factual performance of the product or services they are selling. However the words and pictures which are used often suggest that our lives will be improved in other ways. Eating particular breakfast cereals, or wearing a certain make of shoes, is not really going to enable us to lead more exciting lives, or to meet the person of our dreams.

*continued...*

**45**

# Commercial break (2)

## How do advertisements work?

Most advertisements will only persuade you to try something once. If the product isn't good value, it won't be bought again. You wouldn't buy a bucket with a hole in more than once!

To be really effective an advertisement needs to:
- capture your attention
- arouse your interest
- make you want the product
- help you to remember the name of the product
- prompt you to do something about purchasing the product or service.

## Choosing the right media

Advertisements appear in different forms, each called **media**. For example
- on television and radio
- in newspapers and magazines
- as posters on billboards in the street
- as leaflets or brochures
- as part of exhibitions, displays and publicity stunts or events.

Each media has its own advantages and disadvantages in terms of
- the cost of production
- the cost of repeated exposure
- its effectiveness in reaching the target audience it is aimed at.

Make a list of six different advertising media. For each describe at least two advantages and disadvantages. Try and give real examples wherever you can.

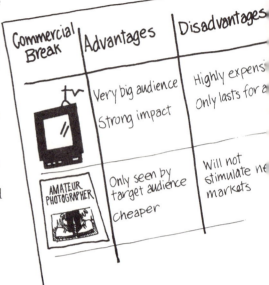

| Commercial Break | Advantages | Disadvantages |
|---|---|---|
| tv | Very big audience / Strong impact | Highly expens / Only lasts for a |
| AMATEUR PHOTOGRAPHER | Only seen by target audience / Cheaper | Will not stimulate ne markets |

Recall and briefly describe some advertisements which have a lot of initial impact on you – those which are maybe colourful, fast-moving, humorous or puzzling, etc.

- To what extent did you actually need the product or service being advertised?
- What general benefits to you were being suggested if you purchased the item? More friends and popularity, perhaps. Or better surroundings, adventure and romance – or improved health, wealth, power, success, and so on.

What was being sold?

How effective were they?

Would I or did I buy the product?

What was the brand name?

## DISCUSSION ISSUES

Do you think the advantages of advertising (products and services are widely available, cheaper and more people are kept in work) outweigh the disadvantages (people are persuaded to buy things they don't really need and feel generally more dissatisfied)?

# Listening in (1)

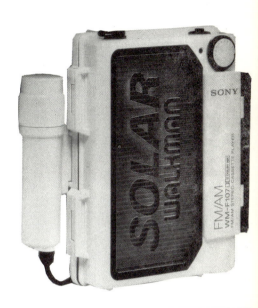

The first Sony 'Walkman' was introduced in 1981. Cassette players had been around for many years, but the size of the speakers and the weight of the batteries needed to drive them meant that they were neither very portable nor usable in public places, such as aeroplanes, trains or in the street.

By using microcircuitry, removing the recording facility and using miniature headphones, the cost and weight were significantly reduced, and the sound became personal.

Sony has continually introduced new models of the 'Walkman', each with new features aimed at slightly different markets.

**MAJOR ASSIGNMENT**

Imagine a leading electronics manufacturer has asked you to undertake a market research programme into personal stereo radio/cassette machines. You will need to discover what models are currently available, how well they perform, and what people think about them.

Using this information you will be able to develop some design proposals for a new model.

### Investigation: what's on the market at present?

First you will need to find out as much as you can about the personal stereos which are currently for sale. Look for information in leaflets, catalogues, magazine articles and advertisements. Ask to look through back copies of *Which* consumer magazine in the local library.

Prepare a market comparison chart to show how different models made by different companies vary in terms of features, performance, weight, looks, reliability, durability, price and overall value for money.

See if you can devise an interesting and unusual system of graphic symbols to use to present the information you discover.

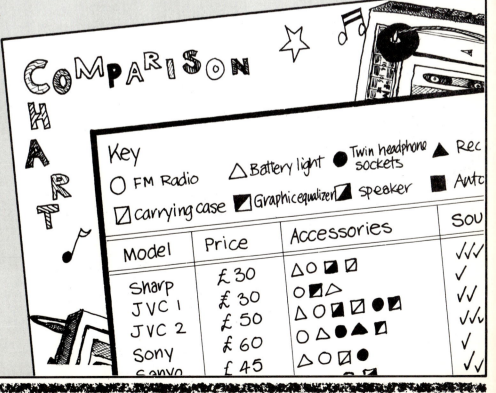

COMPARISON CHART

**Key**
○ FM Radio  △ Battery light  ● Twin headphone sockets  ▲ Rec
☑ carrying case  ◩ Graphic equalizer  ◤ speaker  ■ Auto

| Model | Price | Accessories | Sou |
|---|---|---|---|
| Sharp | £ 30 | △ ○ ◨ ☑ | ✓✓✓ |
| JVC 1 | £ 30 | ○ ◨ △ | ✓ |
| JVC 2 | £ 50 | △ ○ ◨ ☑ ● ◨ | ✓✓ |
| Sony | £ 60 | ○ △ ● ▲ ◤ | ✓✓✓ |
| Sony | £ 45 | △ ○ ☑ ● | ✓ |

*continued ...*

# Listening in (2)

## Product analysis

Make a detailed study of a personal stereo or portable radio. It could be one of your own, or a relative's or friend's. It is important that you do not work just from memory – you will need to have the object in front of you so that you can examine it closely.

Present your analysis as visually as possible on a sheet of A3 paper, including a measured, coloured orthographic drawing of the product.

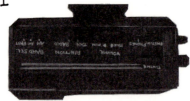

My stereo isn't new at all. I got in 1984 for a birthday present.

I particularly like the fact that it has a radio. This is useful when all the tapes have been played

It also has a graphic equalizer so music can be played just how I like it

The colours are very smart and make it look very desirable and expensive

Overall I am very pleased with the machine's performance and sound quality

There is almost too much power. Volume number 2 or 3 is quite enough

The battery warning light is very useful, though is difficult to see in bright sunlight

# Listening in (3)

## Questionnaire

Organizing a small questionnaire will help you to get a general idea of what sort of things a particular group of people think are important, and will be looking for when choosing which product model to buy.

Find between five and ten friends to ask your questions about their personal stereos or portable radios. It is probably best if you record their answers for them.

You will need to plan the questions you ask very carefully if they are going to be effective in uncovering the information you want to know. Choose about half a dozen questions which will cover the important points. Check they are all relevant.

Some of the questions might only require a yes or no answer, whilst others should give the person being interviewed the chance to talk more openly, such as 'What do you think of ...?' Test a first draft of your questionnaire out on someone to see how well it works and improve it if necessary.

When you've gathered all the information it is important that you draw some overall conclusions from your questionnaire. It may well be possible to effectively represent what you've discovered in a visual way.

*First draft questions to ask*

I said 'Can you hear anything else when you've got your headphones on?'

HONK

Bar chart of colour choice

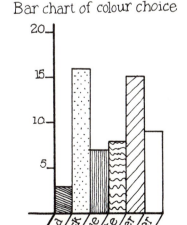

Red, Black, Blue, White, Silver, Other

Pie chart showing % types of music listened to

- 20% Jazz
- 30% Pop
- 15% Classical
- 15% Disco
- 20% Rock

*Conclusions from research*

From the answers I obtained many people seem to want a non-rectangular personal stereo

Ideally it would be smaller and lighter, – an opinion held by nearly all those questioned

The most popular colour was black with silver in close second, although a preference for bright colours was also popular

*continued ...*

# Listening in (4)

## Design development

After reading your market research report, the electronics company asks you to develop some initial ideas for a new personal stereo and/or radio which will appeal to the 9 to 14 age range. They are keen that the overall appearance should be a very distinctive, modern style, and look as original and unconventional as possible.

Begin by looking back at your research and stating:

- the features you think it will need to have
- the price range it is intended for
- any other important specifications.

## First thoughts 💡

Start to develop and sketch out your ideas by:

- experimenting with unusual forms, shapes, colours and patterns
- thinking about what sort of switches and controls might be best
- considering where the controls could be positioned
- exploring different ways in which it might be carried and/or worn.

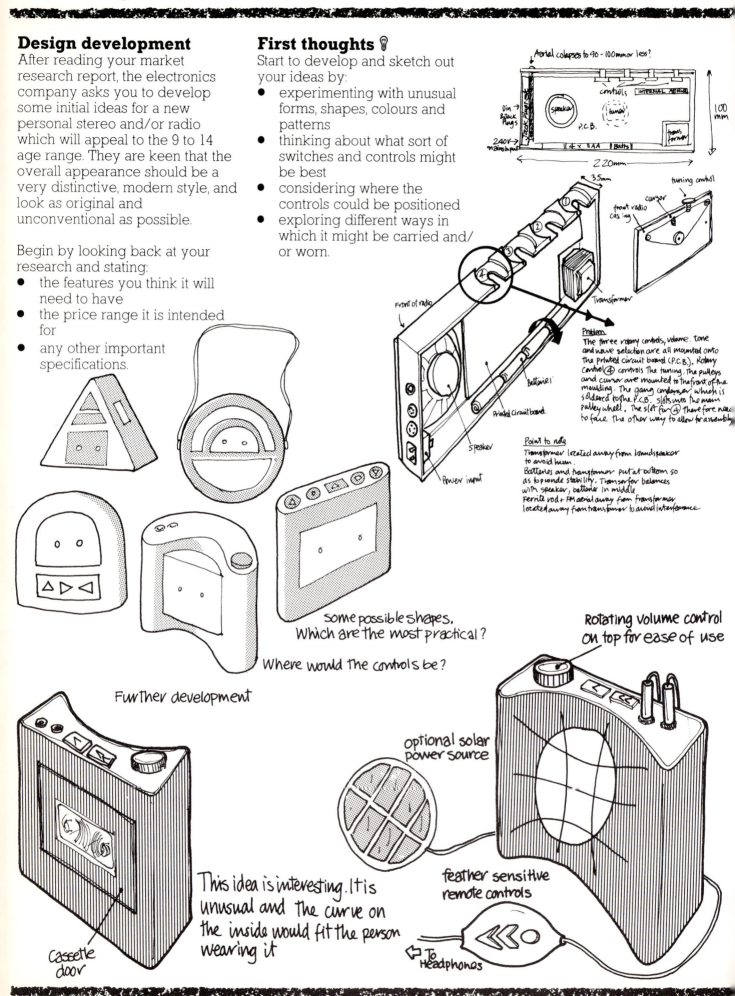

Aerial colapses to 90 - 100 mm or less?

controls   INTERNAL AERIAL

speaker   (tuner)   100 mm

P.C.B.

Din & Jack Plugs

240V mains input   4 x AA Batts   transformer

220mm

35mm

tuning control

cursor

front radio casing

Transformer

Front of radio

Batteries

Printed circuit board.

speaker

Power input

**Problem**
The three rotary controls, volume, tone and wave selection are all mounted onto the printed circuit board (P.C.B). Rotary control ④ controls the tuning, the pulleys and cursor are mounted to the front of the moulding. The gang condenser which is soldered to the P.C.B. slots into the main pulley wheel. The slot for ④ therefore needs to face the other way to allow for assembly

**Point to note**
Transformer located away from loudspeaker to avoid hum.
Batteries and transformer put at bottom so as top provide stability. Transformer balances with speaker, batteries in middle
Ferrite rod + FM aerial away from transformer located away from transformer to avoid interference

some possible shapes. Which are the most practical?

Where would the controls be?

Further development

Rotating volume control on top for ease of use

optional solar power source

feather sensitive remote controls

This idea is interesting. It is unusual and the curve on the inside would fit the person wearing it

Cassette door

To Headphones

## Developing ideas/realization

Check your ideas against your earlier specification statement and select your most promising idea for more detailed development. Finalize its size and shape, making some suggestions for the materials it might be made from, and how the casing could be assembled.

Make a prototype three-dimensional appearance model, and prepare a coloured orthographic drawing.

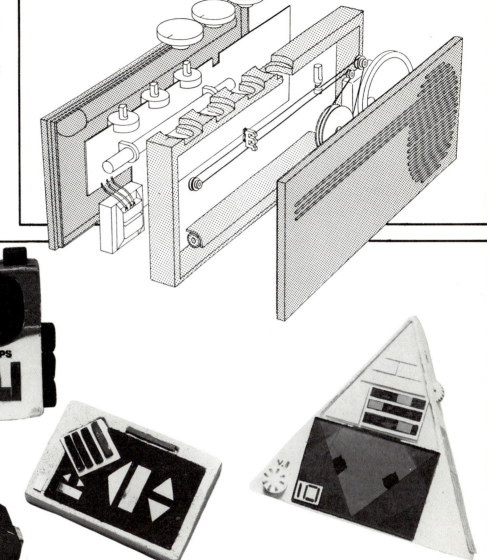

## Final evaluation

Look round carefully at the designs made by other members of your class. How do they differ from yours? Apart from your own, which designs seem to be the most successful? Which would you choose to buy, and why?

What further research and development work would you recommend to be undertaken before the electronics company commits itself to mass-producing the unit?

# Soap opera

# Work, rest and play

**Work** involves physical and/or mental activity for which we are usually rewarded. This is usually by a monetary payment, or some other means, such as an examination certificate, or the feeling that we are helping someone else less fortunate than ourselves.

One way or another the work we do contributes to the survival and well-being of our community. We help others, and they in return help provide our basic needs and wants. Most people want to feel that they have been able to contribute something to the community that supports them.

Not all of us are capable of performing the same tasks. We each have our own unique combination of abilities. It is up to us to discover what we are best at doing and to try and offer our skills to the community.

Work can be difficult and boring, but it can also be challenging and stimulating. It often depends on how well the task has been thought out by the employer, and whether we are well matched to it. And people don't just work for money – they like to be appreciated and regularly thanked for what they have done.

The work we do, and the way we do it, has always been closely related to the use of tools and machines, however simple or complex. Up to now manual work and the completion of straightforward repetitive tasks have kept most of the country's population in full-time employment. Now, however, automation and microtechnology are dramatically changing the type of work which is needed.

Up to twenty or so years ago, teenagers used to prepare themselves for one job which they could normally expect to do for the rest of their working lives. Today young people must be willing and able to change and adapt their skills to perform a variety of different jobs.

Unlike machines we are unable to work for 24 hours a day – we need periods of **rest** and relaxation. **'Playing'** is a very important human activity. When we are playing it doesn't really matter if we make mistakes, and so we can afford to try new things out, and take risks knowing that we can afford to fail.

Young children learn much about the way the world works through 'let's pretend' games and safe constructional toys. But adults need to be able to play too, and through hobbies, special interests and sports they continue to develop their skills and personalities.

## DISCUSSION ISSUES

- How do we decide which work activities deserve more reward than others?
- What are the advantages and disadvantages of working for a very big company, rather than a small local organization?
- How can we ensure that everyone gets a fair share of increased leisure time?

Prepare a number of short group statements which sum up your discussion.

# Job centre

Decide which one of the following proposed industrial/commercial concerns would be most likely to establish itself in your particular locality:

- a leisure centre
- an electronic musical instrument manufacturer
- a nuclear power station
- a hypermarket.

**ASSIGNMENT**

## The recruitment package

Imagine you have been appointed as personnel director. Start by making a list of all the jobs which will be created, from chairperson to cleaners.

The financial adviser reports that you will be able to pay reasonably competitive wages and salaries. In order to attract the best applicants you are also able to offer two of the following benefits:

- low-rent housing
- private health care
- free canteen food
- shorter working hours per week
- a guaranteed 2-year contract
- a percentage of relocation expenses.

Write a short report for the board of directors recommending which benefits should be offered, and why.

Compose a half-page advertisement for the local paper to encourage people to send for further details of employment opportunities.

## The application

Imagine now that you are yourself looking for a new job with the company. Write a short letter to the personnel officer, stating the post you are particularly interested in, and explaining the qualifications, experience and any other qualities you have.

## The interview

You are selected for interview. Working in pairs each take the part of the personnel officer and the prospective employee. Make a list of the questions you would ask as the personnel officer, and the points you would like to get across as the person being interviewed. Allow exactly five minutes for the interview, and then exchange places.

## The domestic help

The other day,
one of our domestic robots went mad,
kissed my dad,
poured marmalade over the videowall,
shampooed the cat,
sugared my mother's hair,
and sat on my sister's knee
(she fell through the chair).

Dad's frantic fiddling with the
control-panel only made matters worse.

It vacuum-cleaned the ceiling,
put the coffee table into the garbage
disposal unit, uncorked a bottle of wine
and poured it gently over the carpet,
then carefully unscrewed its head
and deposited it in Mum's lap.

Mother says
that's the way it is these days:
you can't get the robots you used to.

Adrian Henri

Write a polite but firm letter of complaint to the company who manufactured the robot. Then, as the managing director of the company, write an appropriate reply explaining the production-line difficulties you have recently had.

Carefully read the poem. Draw a coloured cartoon sequence to illustrate the robot and the events which are described.

A. Noid
123 The Road
Anytown
somewhere

The Manager
Complaints Dept
Domebots P.L.C

14-2-89

Dear Sir We have been happily using your domestic robots for over ten years but we are most unsatisfied with your latest model w__ believable tha__

DOMEBOTS
ROBOT HOUSE
SILICON ROAD
DROID TOWN
P.C.B. 1

28-1-89

Dear A. Noid
Thankyou for your recent letter concerning the robot you purchased. I was sorry to hear about the problems you have experienced

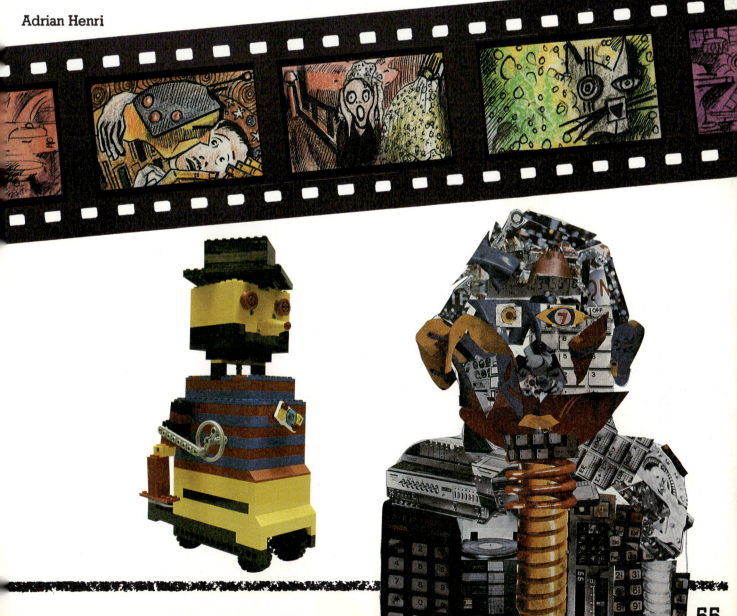

# Robomotion (1)

Design and make a simple working model of a machine or device which imitates a single human limb movement, such as waving, throwing, gripping, etc. This assignment could be undertaken in groups of twos or threes.

Some of the problems of mechanical movement are being solved by looking closely at the way in which living things move – animals, like people and insects.

Designing machines which can take the place of human beings is no easy task. Although progress is being made there is still a long way to go before robots will have the agility, flexibility and intelligence to move in the way in which science fiction films suggest.

*Underwater robot for laying and repairing telephone cables*

## Investigation 🔍

Find out as much as you can about how human limbs move. How many different actions can you think of?

Present a series of drawings to demonstrate the sequence of movement involved in a simple everyday action. Look carefully at the way in which the bones, joints and muscles work together.

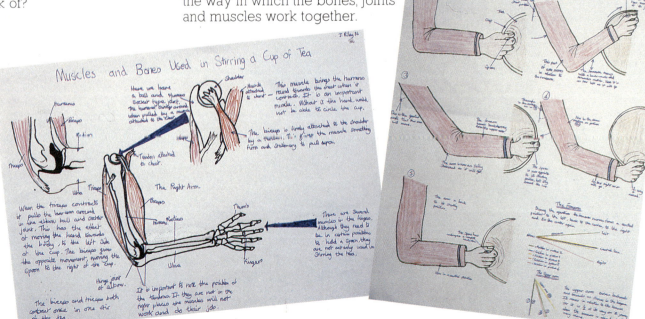

# Robomotion (2)

## First thoughts/developing ideas 💡 ◎

Start with a series of sketch drawings in which you replace the bones, joints and muscles with other components and materials such as strips of wood, hinges, rubber bands and string, etc.

Try making a first working prototype with a technical construction kit if there is one available.

Think carefully about which parts of the device would be made best from everyday materials and which from a construction kit.

Make a final model to demonstrate the action you chose.

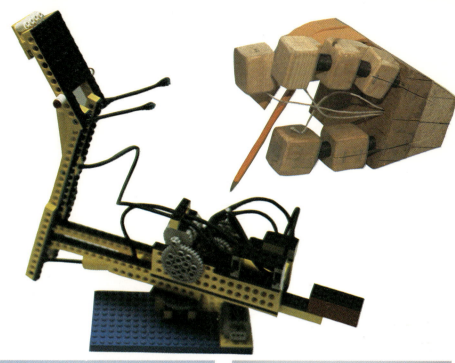

# Fun machines

Fun machines could be described as large-scale devices intended simply to provide pleasure and enjoyment, such as playground structures, amusement arcade machines, fairground rides, etc.

Choose an existing playground or another suitable area near where you live, and design an imaginative play structure for it, based on one of the following themes:

- computer graphics
- mythical creatures
- a particular children's book.

Alternatively it could be a device which can be transported in some way around different sites.

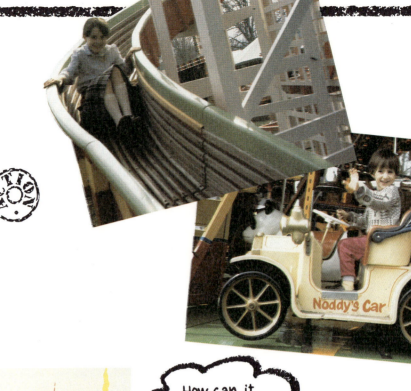

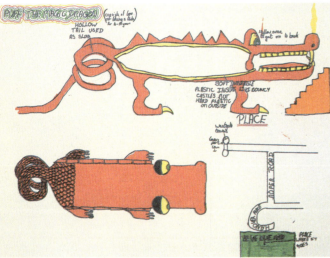

'I began by sketching as many different machines and devices I could think of which were for entertainment, and tried to work out what actually made them fun to use.

I found some illustrations of mythical creatures and worked out one could become the basis of a large playground structure. At the same time I carefully chose an actual site for it.

I was then able to develop my idea in detail, and carefully considered the materials, cost, safety, the age groups that might use it, and what size it would need to be. I also had to take into account the limitations of the site I had selected.

Finally I thought up a name for it, and drew up a coloured presentation sheet to get other people's reactions to it. I also made a small model of the structure in Plasticine.'

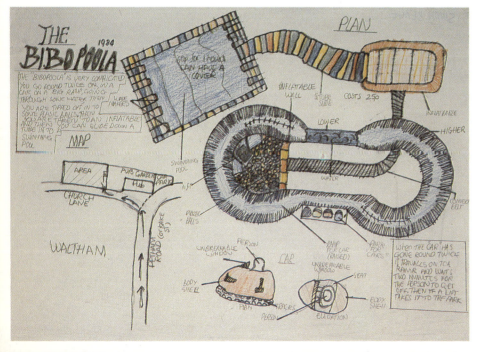

Sketch some ideas out. Choose the most promising and make a simple prototype to find out if it will work.

*How do mechanical toys work?*

*What makes them fun to play with?*

*What should it look like?*

*How can sounds be generated?*

*How can it be made safe?*

Design and make a pull-along toy for a very young child. As it moves along various parts should move too, and it should make unexpected noises.

Observe some young children playing with mechanical toys. Ask them which ones they like best, and why.

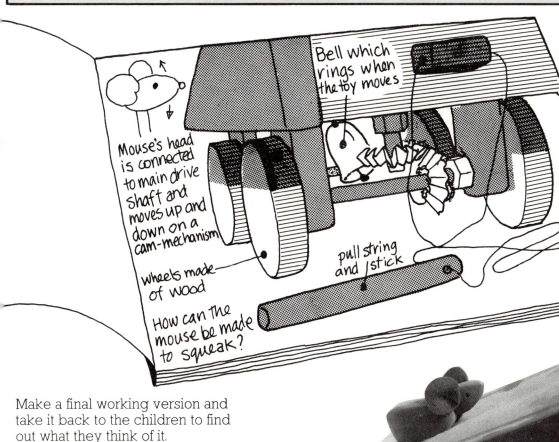

Bell which rings when the toy moves

Mouse's head is connected to main drive shaft and moves up and down on a cam-mechanism

Wheels made of wood

How can the mouse be made to squeak?

pull string and stick

Make a final working version and take it back to the children to find out what they think of it.

If your design was going to be mass-produced what further research and developmental work would need to be done?

# Fun and games (1)

**ASSIGNMENT**

Design and make an original board game which takes no more than an average of twenty minutes to play. It must be based on a theme of some sort.

## Investigation 🔍
Make lists of at least:
- 15 different popular board games
- 15 different card games
- 15 different outdoor games.

Choose one of each type that you either have at home, or can easily borrow. Make a detailed study of each, neatly presented on a sheet of A4 paper. Include a series of very closely observed drawings of the graphics of the board and/ or back of a playing card. Also sketch any three-dimensional playing pieces. Using not more than 75 words, explain as concisely as possible what the game is about and how it is played – the sort of description which might appear on the outside of the box.

Make additional notes on how much you enjoy playing each particular game, and carefully consider what actually makes it **fun**. Also ask other people for their opinions of each game, recording their comments.

Make a collection of visual images (i.e. sketches done by yourself, pictures cut from magazines, graphic symbols, etc.), and verbal references (i.e. descriptive words, names, titles, phrases, sayings, jokes, poems, songs, etc.) based on two of the following:
- horror movies
- space travel
- fashion
- fantastic animals
- super heroes
- cityscape
- fast food
- black and white.

Remember that one of the two themes you choose will come to form the basis of your final board game design.

How many people can play?

What is the idea of the game?

How can it be made interesting?

Are there any special rules?

How does a player finally win?

## First thoughts 💡
Without going into detail, record some ideas for at least six different basic possibilities, referring to your lists of games, detailed game studies and theme sheets. For example, you might start by combining the basis of draughts with a board depicting a galaxy and play pieces being spaceships. Identify the idea you think will be the most successful, writing down the reasons for your choice.

## Developing your ideas ◎

Explore the idea in rough in more detail, starting with sketches and working towards a full-size prototype made from paper.

Don't forget to consider all the basic methods of making games work, such as:
- throwing dice
- picking up instruction cards
- making decisions on directions of movement of playing pieces
- blocking other players
- scoring points on the way.

Test the prototype out by playing and discussing it with other people. Does your game:
- get started quickly enough?
- become dull or repetitive at any stage?
- come to a successful conclusion?

Make clear notes of the changes you decide to make as a result of testing your prototype.

Start to develop and refine the description of the playing instructions and rules.

Work out how you can make the board look as visually interesting as possible by incorporating colourful images from your theme sheet. Use some of your verbal references to help co-ordinate playing cards and locations on the board.

## Final realization ✌

Construct and prepare the art work for the final version in thin card as neatly and accurately as possible. How could any card playing pieces be made to stand up?

Include the playing instructions and rules, which must include a high proportion of explanatory diagrams.

## The people game

Design a simple board game to be played in a specific space in your school. The playing pieces are to be members of your class.

# Shelter

Shelter is a basic human need. Animals often have their own in-built protection, but human beings need to be able to shelter from the elements. As well the extremes of weather, we sometimes also need to be protected from insects and wild animals, and from each other.

Every day we use many different types of shelter in different circumstances. What can each of the following protect us from?
- a tree
- a bus shelter
- the garden wall
- a phone booth

Can you think of some examples of the ways in which animals are better adapted to survival from the effects of the weather and predators?

## Home sweet home (1)

The most common form of human shelter is, of course, a house. Unlike the nests or burrows made by some animals, a house is permanent. It is somewhere that we know we and our families will be safe, and that will keep our possessions secure. It is somewhere we can be ourselves and make our own choices about the way in which we want to live.

But not all houses are the same. The layout and appearance of dwellings around the world is influenced by the locally available tools and materials, the climate, the way of life of the population, financial limitations and the traditional ways of building.

Find out as much as you can about the way in which the following types of dwellings are made and used:
- the yurt (central Asia)
- the teppee (American Indian)
- the igloo (Eskimo)
- the pueblo (Mexican deserts)
- the bedouin tent (Arabia).

Find out about the ways in which birds make nests, rabbits make burrows and bees make hives. What similarities are there to the ways humans design their shelters?

# Home sweet home (2)

## How have houses changed in this country?

The design of houses has changed very little in hundreds of years. Although modern houses may at first look very different to those built last century, inside they are surprisingly similar in their layout and use of spaces. Unlike many domestic products, houses are built to last a long time. What has changed is some of the materials they are built from, the methods of construction, and the sophistication of the way in which energy is supplied and controlled.

Thirty years ago a lot of people thought that building high-rise blocks of flats would solve the housing problem. In what ways have they proved to be wrong?

*Slum clearance in the 1960's*

### DISCUSSION ISSUES

- How do houses need to change in the future?
- Are more new houses needed, or should old ones be improved?
- Do we need more larger houses, or smaller ones?
- How can dwellings be made so that it is easier to alter or extend them?
- How long should a house last for?

*A vision of the future*

# My house (1)

## What does your house look like?

Draw a sketch elevation of the front of your house from memory. Don't attempt to make it three-dimensional in any way, and don't use rulers or straight edges. Think carefully about:

- the arrangement of the rooms and passageways inside
- where the windows and doors should be
- the height of the floors and roof
- the materials it is built from.

Go and stand outside your house with your completed drawing in your hand and compare it closely to the reality You might be surprised at some of the mistakes you have made. Make a written note of all the differences you can spot, and re-sketch the same view more accurately.

## Personalization

Although houses in a row often look very similar to each other, very few will be absolutely identical. People like to make their homes feel special and in some way individual – a personalized reflection of their own particular needs, tastes and the things they value. To achieve this they change the details – a different front door or porch, a brightly painted gate, or an extension maybe.

Has **your** home been personalized? Look closely at the:

- wall surfaces
- windows
- doorways
- garden
- gates
- fences

and compare them with those of other houses in the street. Look out for variations in materials, colours, patterns and decorative objects. Sketch what you see and add notes to indicate what you think about what has been done. Have any of them become eyesores, or spoilt the overall character of the street?

Apart from their homes and gardens, what other things do people like to personalize?

# My house (2)

## How does your house work?

A famous architect once described a house as a 'machine for living in'. He meant that as well as being a pleasant place to be in, it also had to perform certain tasks efficiently.

Imagine how it would feel to be the house you live in at present. What would you like to say about the state of health of your energy systems, the condition of your outward appearance, and some of the interesting things which have happened to you? And what do you think of your occupants?

Re-draw the picture using a picture of your house, and substituting its replies to the questions in the speech bubbles.

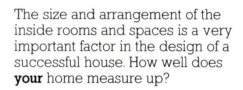

The size and arrangement of the inside rooms and spaces is a very important factor in the design of a successful house. How well does **your** home measure up?

Start by drawing rough floor plans of your house from memory. Think very carefully about the size and shape of each room and its position relative to other rooms and passageways. Add in where you think the doors and windows are, and also the main items of furniture, such as settees, beds, wardrobes, etc.

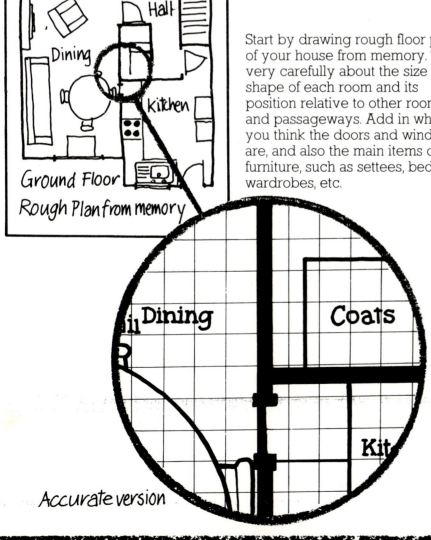

Then go and stand just inside your front door with the completed rough plans in your hand. Use the plans just like a map, and walk round the house comparing your drawings with the actual layout.

- Are the doorways and windows large enough, and in the right position?
- Are the passageways wide enough?
- Is the furniture correctly drawn?

You need not measure all the distances very accurately, but you might find it helpful sometimes to pace out the lengths of things for comparison.

Using a different colour make a note of the differences you find on your memory plan. Re-draw a revised, neater set of plans, adding in wall thicknesses, and using conventional drawing symbols to indicate doors, windows and so on. You will need to choose a suitable scale, and might find it easier to work on squared paper.

*continued …*

# My house (3)

## A functional diagram of your house

Look back at the floor plans you have drawn of your house. In rough, draw each floor again, except this time in a very much simpler way, more as a diagram. Instead of representing the actual space, just use a circle instead. The size of each circle should be the same, and the distance between them, or their position next to each other is not important.

Where it is possible to move directly from one space to another, draw in a line to link the two together. Don't forget the front and back door too.

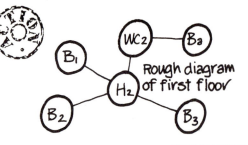

Rough diagram of first floor

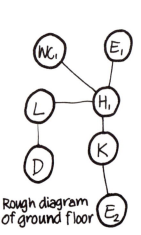

Rough diagram of ground floor

Put a letter into each circle to name it, and add in a key. Draw a neat version of the diagram, this time joining the floors together with a connecting line (the staircase).

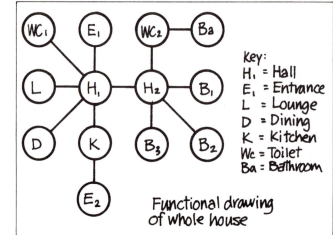

key:
H₁ = Hall
E₁ = Entrance
L = Lounge
D = Dining
K = Kitchen
Wc = Toilet
Ba = Bathroom

Functional drawing of whole house

## Axonometric

Architects often use **axonometric** drawings and sketches to help them represent the spaces and places they are creating. They are quicker and easier to draw than perspectives: all you need is the basic plan and a general idea of the height of the rooms – and a little practice ....

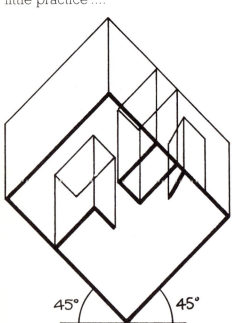

45°     45°

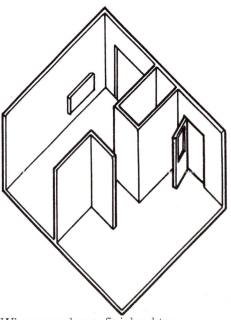

When you have finished try drawing an **axonometric** of the outside of your house.

Choose a part of your house – preferably two rooms and part of the corridor that joins them together – and produce a neat axonometric drawing. Work it out in rough first, and decide which walls to cut away or leave out. Add in the main items of furniture. Think carefully about the colours and textures you use.

- Draw the plan out in pencil, tilted at 45 degrees.
- At each corner draw a vertical line upwards until it looks to be about the right height.
- Join the tops of the vertical lines.
- Remove all the lines which would be hidden.
- Add in the wall thicknesses.

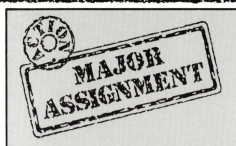

One morning you and your family receive some bad news. A new by-pass is to be built and you have been informed that it will be necessary to completely demolish your existing house.

However there is some good news, too. The local council are going to compensate you by providing a vacant plot of land quite close by in an area of local beauty, and enough money to enable you to have built the house you and your family have always wanted ...

So what will your ideal home be like? Make a list for each member of your family of the features and facilities you think they would want. Start by thinking about the things which are inconvenient or unsatisfactory about your present home.

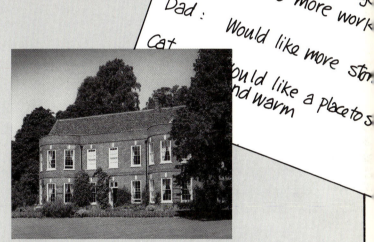

Notes

Myself: I would like a big ... put all my things

Mum: Needs more work ...

Dad: Would like more stor...

Cat ...ould like a place to s... ...nd warm

*Dream houses?*

*continued ...*

# All change (2)

Next day, though, your family receives more bad news when they discover that, because the plot of land is in a conservation area, local planning regulations insist that any new houses:

- can only be one storey high
- must not exceed 150 square metres.

You will now need to review your list of requirements. Most of them will probably have to go, leaving you with just the essential spaces. Think about how your family's needs might change over the next five to ten years – maybe an older brother or sister is likely to move out, or an elderly relative might need to move in?

A functional Diagram of My House
(and changes I would like to make)

Key

12m² (H) – HALL (1)
16m² (K) – KITCHEN
12m² (D) – Dining Room
25m² (L) – LIVING ROOM
}  LOWER FLOOR

16m² (B1) – BEDROOM 1
8m² (H) – Hall (2)
20m² (B2) – BEDROOM 2
4m² (WC) – TOILET (2)
12m² (Ba) – BATHROOM
}  UPPER FLOOR

(FD) – FRONT DOOR
125m² (BD) – BACK DOOR
+       (G) – GREENHOUSE

↓
changes
9m² STUDY (S)
10m² LIBRARY (Lib)
────────────
144m² TOTAL

Downstairs with changes

## First thoughts 💡

Work out roughly how many square metres are needed for each space. To do this you will have to find out how big some of your existing rooms are. For example, if your present kitchen measures roughly 3 metres by 4 metres, then it occupies 12 square metres ($m^2$). In your new house you might decide to make this a little bigger or smaller, depending on what you think is needed. No room should be smaller than $3\,m^2$.

When you have worked out the size for each room, add up the total to check it does not exceed $150\,m^2$. You may need to go back and adjust the individual room sizes until they reach an appropriate total. At this stage allow about $15\,m^2$ for passageways.

Then go back to the functional diagram you prepared on page 66. This should form the basis of your new layout, as everything is now confined to one floor.

Re-draw the diagram adding in extra circles to represent new spaces and removing any rooms which are no longer needed. Make any necessary changes to the connection lines to improve circulation.

# All change (3)

Next change the circles back into rectangular rooms and passageways and see how you can make them roughly fit together, making sure you follow the rules below.

Experiment by making the rooms slightly different shapes. As your plan develops try and form the rooms into an overall basic house shape.

## Some rules

- No room (except for a toilet) can be smaller than 3 m².
- A separate toilet should be at least 2 m².
- All rooms must have natural light – i.e. contain an outside wall.
- The length of the longer side of a room should not be greater than twice the shorter size.
- A bathroom is not allowed to lead directly off a living room or kitchen.
- All corridors/passageways must be at least 1 m wide.
- All doorways must be at least 1 m wide.

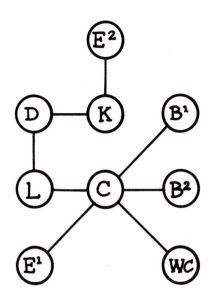

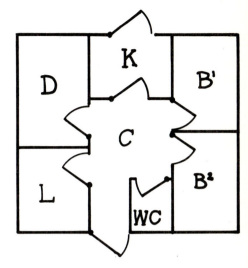

Most house plans are based on shapes like these:

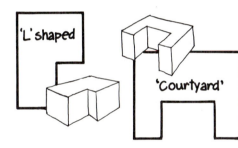

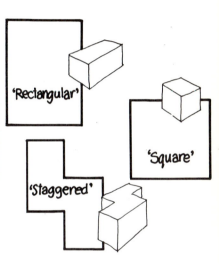

'L' shaped

'Courtyard'

'Rectangular'

'Square'

'Staggered'

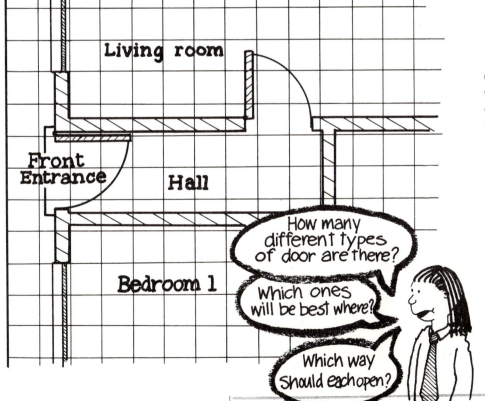

Living room

Front Entrance

Hall

Bedroom 1

How many different types of door are there?

Which ones will be best where?

Which way should each open?

## Getting down to details: wall thicknesses, windows and doors

You might find it useful to work on grid paper to help you develop your final plan. A grid scale of 20 mm = 1 m (i.e. 1:50) is a good size to choose.

Round the outside of your plan you will need to add on an external wall thickness of 200 mm. Inside you will have to make wall thicknesses 100 mm, which will make each space slightly smaller.

Work out where you think windows should be positioned, and how wide they should be. Windows cannot be placed on corners.

continued ...

# All change (4)

## Furniture

Think about where each piece of your present furniture might fit. You must use existing items as far as possible, though you may decide to get rid of some items if space is short, or to purchase new pieces if your family does not already have them.

Make sure that you provide enough space to move round each item of furniture – at least a metre.

## Final realization ⚒

When everything is sorted out, draw out a very neat plan on plain A2 or A3 paper. Add in realistic colour and texture as appropriate. Don't forget to neatly label each room. If you have time draw a section of your new house in axonometric projection.

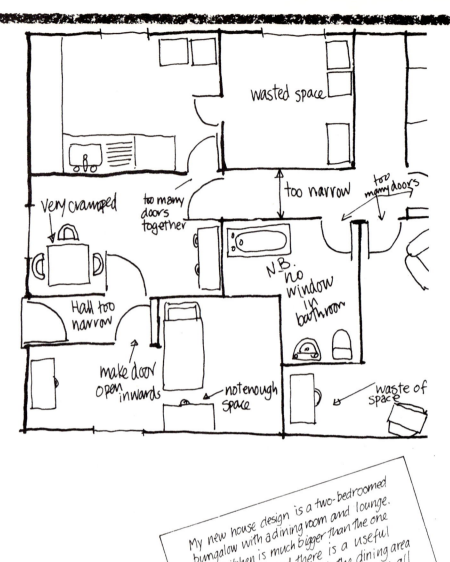

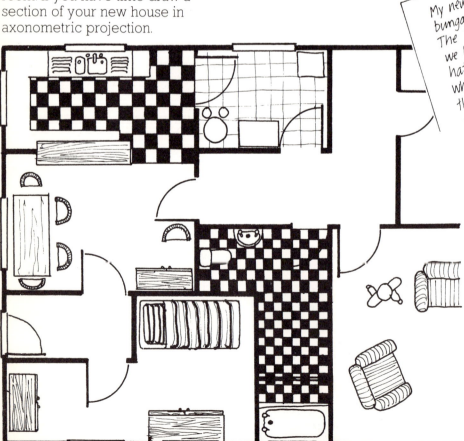

My new house design is a two-bedroomed bungalow with a dining room and lounge. The kitchen is much bigger than the one we have now and there is a useful hatch/bar connecting into the dining area which saves walking into the kitchen all the time. A separate room for the washing machine and freezer is next to the kitchen. There are tiles in the bathroom ... carpets, sofas and tables ... living room is bigger ... before

## Evaluation ⚖

Compare your final design with the house you live in at present. What main advantages would your new design have for you and your family? Are there any disadvantages?

Work out and write down the particular features you would draw to each member of your family's attention in order to convince them of the value of your plan.

Show them your work and see if they do approve of your ideas. Record their comments in your final evaluation.

## On site

The site for your new home is 50 m by 75 m, but this has to accommodate a number of other houses as well. There is a splendid view to the east, and garden areas should preferably not face north as they will not get as much direct sunlight. There will be one entry to the site for vehicles from the southern corner, with a road/pavement width of 15 m.

Work in a group of five. Discuss amongst yourselves and note everyone's preferences for the size and location of their gardens. Then, work out where you would place each house on the site, the shape of each garden plot and the positioning of the drive and pathways.

Work on A3 or A4 paper. To help you explore different possible basic layouts you should cut out scaled-down shapes of each person's house as a template to draw round. Don't forget to number each variation and to note down its good and bad points. Instead of using card templates, a microcomputer could be very effectively used if you have a suitable graphics program.

When you have discovered the best arrangement you should each draw out a final neat labelled version.

Yet more bad news! The local council now wish to squeeze three extra houses onto the same site.

Re-group into eights. Everyone should now attempt to re-design their earlier layout, incorporating the extra houses. There may need to be major changes to ensure that everyone is happy with their garden spaces and general access.

In your final evaluation you should comment on how much more difficult the task became when the extra houses were added in.

# Information

There was once a time when our early ancestors could remember past events, but had not yet developed a way of communicating such information to each other. Eventually cave drawings and word of mouth became sophisticated enough to pass on memories and important instructions. Written letters and words gradually replaced visual symbols to record ideas and information.

The first books were laboriously copied by hand. Mechanical printing presses were developed in the seventeenth century, but did not have any real impact on the speed and quantity of everyday communication until the late nineteenth century, largely because many people still could not read.

It is only during the last hundred years that new inventions in electronic communication technology has made things possible today which our grandparents would have found hard to imagine when they were young.

Just fifty years ago, for example, black and white television sets were large pieces of furniture which could only be afforded by the well-off. And it was only just over twenty years ago when the first live satellite TV pictures were transmitted.

What all these inventions have achieved is to drastically increase the amount of **information** which can be stored, and the speed at which it can be recalled and communicated.

Within the next few years electronic communication devices will continue to become even smaller, cheaper and more capable than they are today. They will begin to have an even greater effect on the quality of our everyday lives.

## Communication devices

How many common devices can you think of which use electronic means of handling information? Write a list, and try and find at least twenty. Find pictures in old magazines and look round at home and at school, making sketches of examples you see. Assemble them into a collage on A3 paper.

Talk to your parents and older relatives about how they feel about new information and communication devices. What inventions have amazed them? How well do they understand how they work? How dependent on them have they become?

## DISCUSSION ISSUES

● What potential advantages and disadvantages are there in likely future developments in communication technology?

● Who will benefit the most from new communications devices?

● When will it be better to use non-electronic means of communication?

● What sort of messages will people want to send?

# Communication evaluation

Obtain at least two or three examples of **one** of the following items of two-dimensional information design:

- advertising leaflets for similar products or services (e.g. cars, savings accounts, etc.)
- packages from a range of similar products (e.g. toothpaste, cornflakes, etc.)
- teenage magazines.

Describe the examples you have obtained using a mixture of words and coloured sketches which show some of the details of the graphics which have been used. Go on to prepare a short comparative report on how well you think each of your examples has been designed.

Look back at the list of 'evaluation' words on page 8.

## Describing the information

- What information is it trying to communicate?
- Who are the messages intended for?
- What has been described by words, and what by which visual means?
- What colours have been used?
- What different styles and sizes of lettering have been used?

## Evaluating the information ⚖

- Does it tell readers what they need to know?
- Are the messages clear enough?
- Is the layout easy to follow?
- Is it visually appealing?
- How good is the quality of paper or card it has been printed on?

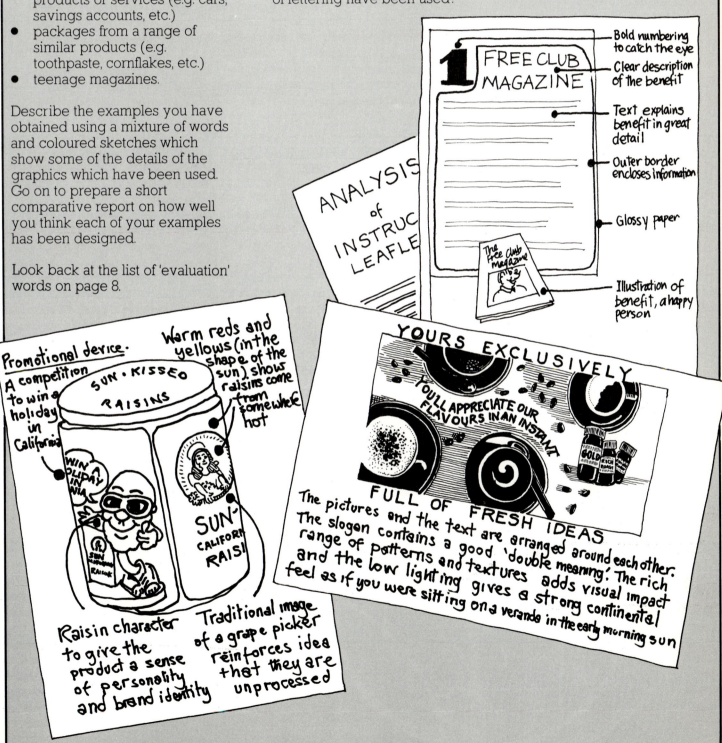

ANALYSIS of INSTRUC LEAFLE

1 FREE CLUB MAGAZINE

- Bold numbering to catch the eye
- Clear description of the benefit
- Text explains benefit in great detail
- Outer border encloses information
- Glossy paper
- Illustration of benefit, a happy person

The Free Club magazine

Promotional device. A competition to win a holiday in California

Warm reds and yellows (in the shape of the sun) show raisins come from somewhere hot

SUN·KISSED RAISINS

WIN A HOLIDAY IN NIA

SUN CALIFORNIA RAISI

Raisin character to give the product a sense of personality and brand identity

Traditional image of a grape picker reinforces idea that they are unprocessed

YOURS EXCLUSIVELY

YOU'LL APPRECIATE OUR FLAVOURS IN AN INSTANT

FULL OF FRESH IDEAS

The pictures and the text are arranged around each other. The slogan contains a good 'double meaning'. The rich range of patterns and textures adds visual impact and the low lighting gives a strong continental feel as if you were sitting on a veranda in the early morning sun

# Person to person (1)

Imagine you have been asked to design a personal communication device for use as a prop in a science fiction film set in the year 2000. Make a full-size model of your final proposal.

*Where could it be worn?*

*What should it look like?*

*What functions will it need to incorporate?*

*What size can it be? What weight?*

*How might it be powered?*

## First thoughts

Look back at your list and collage sheet of electronic communication devices.

Experiment by drawing different combinations of various devices and components. Do lots of sketches, and don't worry if at first they look odd or unlikely.

Choose two or three of your most promising ideas and develop them further.

Don't forget to add explanatory notes and colour to your drawings!

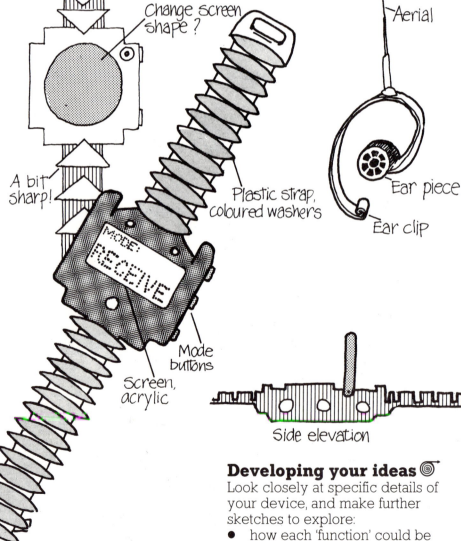

Change screen shape?

A bit sharp!

Aerial

Ear piece

Ear clip

Plastic strap, coloured washers

MODE: RECEIVE

Mode buttons

Screen, acrylic

Side elevation

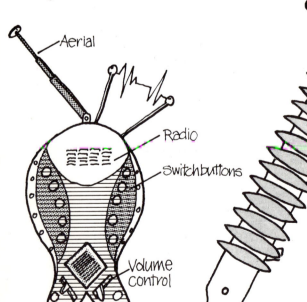

Aerial

Radio

Switch buttons

Volume control

## Developing your ideas

Look closely at specific details of your device, and make further sketches to explore:

- how each 'function' could be operated
- where the switches and controls should be placed
- what size it will need to be.

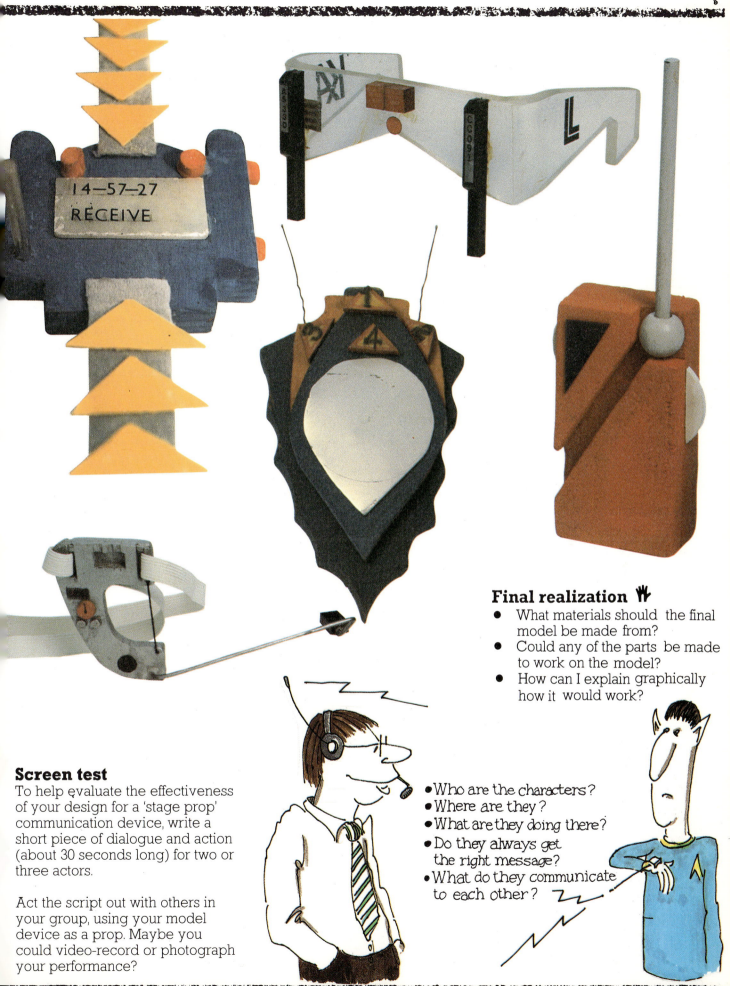

**14—57—27**
**RECEIVE**

### Final realization

- What materials should the final model be made from?
- Could any of the parts be made to work on the model?
- How can I explain graphically how it would work?

### Screen test

To help evaluate the effectiveness of your design for a 'stage prop' communication device, write a short piece of dialogue and action (about 30 seconds long) for two or three actors.

Act the script out with others in your group, using your model device as a prop. Maybe you could video-record or photograph your performance?

- Who are the characters?
- Where are they?
- What are they doing there?
- Do they always get the right message?
- What do they communicate to each other?

# It's not what you say …

ASSIGNMENT

Write down a number of situations in which someone needs to send a message to someone else

For example:

'Happy Birthday' to a relative in Australia

'We're Open' - a new take-away in town wanting customers

'Where you can park in town' advice for the motorist

For each situation draw up an illustrated chart to show the various advantages and disadvantages of at least three completely different ways in which the message could be sent

HOW...?

How long will the message take to get there?

Will the message be expected?

How reliable is the method?

How much does each method cost?

Will the message be clear when it is received?

How easy is it to....

.... prepare and send?

Experiment

Try sending a real message to someone in three different ways. Record what you did, which method worked best and why.

# Am I making myself clear?

There are many different ways of using codes and signals to enable information to be sent between two people. Look in the library and find out more about ancient coding systems such as Morse code, semaphore, etc. Prepare an illustrated A3 sheet recording your research.

Devise and make an unusual means of sending a simple one-word message which will be secret to yourself and the person you transmit it to. Make your solution in some sort of three-dimensional form, using a combination of any materials available to you.

Which ideas will work best in 3D?

What different materials could be used?

Could electronic circuits be incorporated?

# Mind over matter

Design and conduct an experiment to test your powers of telepathic communication. Make a series of shapes and discover how much information about them you can 'transmit' to a friend in another room who can't see them.

What shapes could be used?
How many?
How can the results be recorded?
How much can be put down to chance?

# Communication breakdown

Imagine **you** are the television set which you watch at home. Draw a cartoon which reveals what you saw and heard one evening when there was a power cut.

How well did we cope without them?

Which electronic devices wouldn't work?

Which T.V. programmes did we miss most?

How did I feel about it? Was I glad it happened?

# Symbols and logos (1)

Symbols are simplified visual images, intended to communicate information in a way which is easier and quicker to understand. Logos perform the same task, except that they are based on letters of the alphabet, instead of pictures.

Most commercial organizations use visual symbols to enable the public to rapidly identify the name of the company offering particular goods or services. The best symbols are simple and distinctive, but still manage to say a great deal about the particular company they identify.

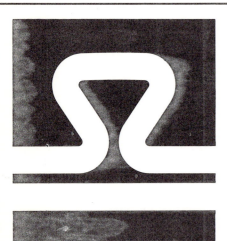

### Sealink symbol
This distinctive symbol illustrates many aspects of the service being offered. The shape might be read as:
- the braid round the jacket cuff of an officer
- the plan of a harbour
- an elevation of a capstan
- the cross-section of a boat.

As well as all these things, it is also based on the initial letters of the company.

Can you identify which company uses this symbol?

## ASSIGNMENT

From memory draw at least twelve different symbols and logos, including their colours. When you have finished find examples of the actual design and carefully compare them with your drawings. Make a note of any differences you discover in shape, arrangement, proportion and colour.

Make a collection of company symbols cut from advertisements in old magazines or from packages, etc.

Divide your collection up under the following headings:
- those based on the use of the initial letters of the company name (e.g. BHS, AA)
- those based on writing out the full name of the company using a distinctive style of lettering (e.g. Boots, Ford)
- those which include an illustration of the product or service being offered (e.g. the Woolmark, British Steel)
- those based on a decorative shape or pattern or an illustration of the company name (e.g. BMW, Penguin Books).

You will find that many could be placed under more than one heading – in which case put them into the group which you have fewest of.

Neatly cut them out and stick them down onto A4 or A3 paper. Conduct a small survey to discover how easily and quickly they can be identified and named.

Then label each, saying how effective you think it is.

## Personal identity

Design a symbol or logo to represent yourself.

Start by drawing out in rough at least six completely different possibilities involving different combinations of:

- your initials
- your full first or surname
- simplified illustrations of your interests or hobbies
- an abstract pattern which you feel represents your personality in some way.

By each write your comments on how effective you think it is. Choose the approach you consider to be best, and develop the idea in a great deal more detail.

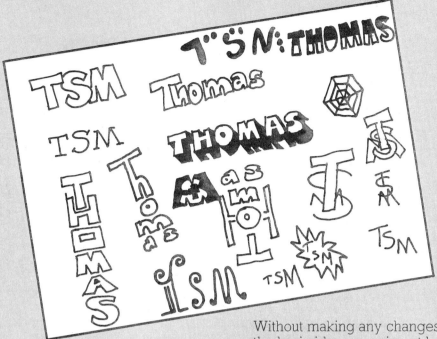

Without making any changes to the basic idea, experiment by trying some of the following transformations:

- make some elements larger or smaller
- repeat some parts to make a pattern
- allow different shapes to overlap
- reverse black lines and areas of white
- make some elements three-dimensional
- use different combinations of colours
- simplify the design as much as possible.

If you have the facilities some of these experiments could be done very effectively on a microcomputer.

Finalize your design and draw it out very neatly. Add a minimum of dimensions and written instructions and exchange with a partner to see if you can make an identical copy without having to explain them further to each other.

If possible get a number of copies reduced to various sizes on a photocopier and cut and paste one onto another sheet of paper to make a personal letter-heading. Other copies could be fixed onto some of your belongings.

# Transport

Our increasing ability to move from place to place quickly and comfortably has made a great deal of difference to the way in which we live our everyday lives.

In prehistoric times, early humans could do little more than throw the animals they had just killed over their backs and stagger slowly back to their caves. Then for many centuries the horse and cart was the only readily available form of transport. Many people never travelled very far beyond the village they were born in.

Since then we have invented the engine and discovered how to float, hover and fly in order to get to work, to the shops, to see friends and relatives, and to go on holidays.

There are many reasons why we need to be able to travel from place to place and many ways of undertaking our journey. Our choice of transport will depend on:

- how quickly we need to travel
- how safe and comfortable we want to feel
- how much we can afford
- how much luggage we have to take with us.

However, the roadways, train system and airways are becoming more and more crowded and the cost of travel is often considerable. And the fuel which is needed uses up our resources at an alarming rate, polluting the atmosphere at the same time.

## DISCUSSION ISSUES

- How many different forms of transport do you use each week?
- Do you enjoy travelling?
- Are there any alternatives to present types of cars and aeroplanes?
- Should public transport be improved instead of facilities for private transport?

# Getting around

### ASSIGNMENTS

How many different devices have you ever used to travel from one place to another? What other forms of transport do people use? Think of at least thirty examples and sketch them on a sheet of A3 paper, grouping your ideas together under the heading **air, land, sea** and **water**.

Choose five different examples of methods of transport and produce a chart to compare how each performs. Consider speed, safety, comfort, cost and capacity.

### Which way to go?

Imagine you are a witch on a broomstick. What would be the various advantages and disadvantages of such a means of travel? Would you prefer a magic carpet, or not?

Compose a spell to instruct your broomstick where you want to go and how you expect it to behave.

Write a classified advertisement to appear in the 'Broomsticks for Sale' section of your local paper.

# Saver return

An elderly couple need to get from your house to Hyde Park Corner in London and to the pier of the nearest seaside resort to where you live. Work out for them precisely:

- the **cheapest** method of getting there
- the **fastest** method of getting there
- the **easiest** when carrying two heavy suitcases.

You will need to find out about the times and costs of different combinations of trains, buses and maybe even aeroplanes. Private cars or bicycles may not be used, but short taxi rides are allowed.

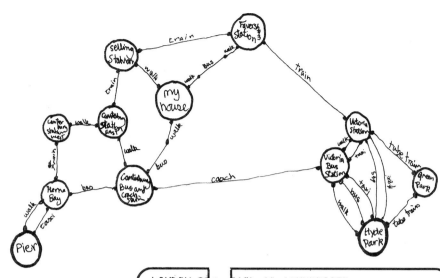

## LONDON BY RAIL AS ADVERTISED

Make a full presentation of the three alternatives using maps and plans, graphic symbols, colour coding, different scales and so on to provide clear instructions. Include any other information and advice you think might be helpful.

If possible show your work to an elderly person to check that it can be easily understood. Make a note of any comments they make. Ask them about how they think and feel about travel today compared to when they were young.

# Terminus (1)

## ASSIGNMENT

Moving large numbers of people as quickly as possible around towns and cities is a complex problem. A combination of different types of transportation devices are often needed, and being able to transfer easily between them is important. And what else is needed when there is some time to spare, or if we are very young, old, or have a lot of luggage to carry?

Your local bus company is proposing to construct a major new bus station in a nearby city. Within the building there is to be a large central concourse area through which all passengers will have to pass. Imagine you have been asked to design the shape and layout of the concourse, which must not be bigger than 200m².

- Where will the bus station be sited?
- What other transport systems will it need to connect in with?

## Investigation

Make a study of your nearest main bus station:

- How do passengers find out which bus stop to wait at?
- What do they do while they wait?
- What other people apart from passengers use or work in the bus station?
- How well organized is the layout?

## Developing ideas

Draw up a matrix like the one below to work out which facilities need to be closest together.

Give each of the six most important facilities a letter reference and enter it onto a matrix grid.

## First thoughts

List all the facilities which you think will be needed in the bus station as a whole. Identify those which will be within the central area, and those which will lead directly off it.

Decide which are the six most important main facilities in the concourse.
Work out roughly how much space each will need to occupy, remembering that they all have to fit into a space no bigger than 200m², and that at least 40m² will need to be provided for circulation.

| | A Café | B Telephones | C Toilets | D Bus area | Tic... |
|---|---|---|---|---|---|
| A Café | | 1 | 1 | 2 | 1 |
| B Telephones | | | 0 | 2 | 1 |
| C Toilets | | | | 2 | ( |
| D Bus area | | | | | |
| E Tickets | | | | | |

- If you think it is not necessary to have facilities A and B close together in the concourse area fill in the top A/B square with a 0.
- If it would be quite a good idea to have A and B close together, though not essential, put a 1 in the square.
- If it is highly desirable to have A and B next to each other, put a 2 in the square.

Repeat this process for A and C, A and D and so on until the top half is completed.

Set the letters A to F out in a circle as shown. Refer back to the matrix you completed and draw a line in between each pair of letters with a '2' relationship. Draw a broken line between pairs with a '1' relationship.

Using a series of further diagrams, try and find an arrangement of letters in which none of the full lines cross, and, if possible, none of the broken lines.

Your final diagram should form the basis of the layout for the area. Now think about each letter as a space, roughly the size you worked out earlier, and all the spaces as the complete three-dimensional concourse.

Description of the waiting Area

'At the main entrance is a slope, rather than steps, as it is more convenient for elderly or disabled people.

There are public telephones in three key places, and clocks situated around the building along with litter and fire extinguishers.

You can buy souvenirs, sweets, drinks, tourist guides, and other small items in the shop and refreshment area which are both near the seating area and main entrance.

The building faces south, allowing the waiting area to be lit and heated by the sun.'

# Holiday exchange

It is the height of the holiday season. The airport terminal is crowded. Seats on flight 409 have been double-booked, and a group of frustrated travellers are gathered round the check-in desk. Who's to blame? Is it human error, technical failure, or both? And how is the problem going to be solved?

Working in a group, each choose one of the following roles. Think carefully about how your character feels about the situation, and what they will say and do. Then improvise to find out what happens ....

## Passenger couple A and B
You are most irate. Secretly you enjoy a good scene, and this looks like a good opportunity to make as much fuss as you possibly can. Compensation in the form of a more expensive holiday than the one you booked is what you are really after.

## Passenger couple C and D
You are a woman travelling with your five-year-old child. You have been looking forward to your holiday for a long time, but your main concern is that you are six months' pregnant. You get tired very easily and need plenty of rest.

## Passenger E
You do not wish to draw too much attention to yourself as you are actually smuggling watches, and you suspect you are being followed. Unfortunately your contact is expecting you first thing in the morning, and if you can't get a flight the deal will be off.

## Holiday firm representative
Good old Head Office have got it wrong again. You are not empowered to offer compensation, only an alternative flight or a full refund. You might be able to arrange a private car to meet the later flight 411, but the two passengers will probably then have to travel by train to their original holiday destination. Unfortunately your computer link doesn't seem to be working properly, so you can't at present actually confirm these arrangements.

## Check-in officer
This is all you need at the end of a long hard day. There are two spare first class seats on flight 411 to a nearby airport. Although 411 is scheduled to depart shortly it is likely to be delayed for about five hours. Which passengers are you going to give the seats to?

# Airport survival kit

A manufacturing company has 10 000 spare plastic boxes measuring 350 by 250 by 150 mm. They have decided to use them as the basis of **airport survival kits** which can be sold on the spot to passengers facing delays of between 6 and 24 hours.

You have been asked to advise what items the kit should contain, and to produce the graphic design for a cardboard sleeve to be placed round the plastic box.

- How much will the items cost?
- How will they fit into the box?
- What information needs to be on the packaging?

# On the run

In order to escape to a neutral country, a secret agent needs to cross a level distance of 200 metres. Unfortunately the spy has been injured and is unable to walk. In the spy's hideout there is a basic workshop and a limited selection of tools and mainly scrap materials.

Design and make a model of a device to travel and carry the secret agent to safety. Scaled down, your model will need to travel about 10 metres. Begin by working in a group of five, each choosing one of the following as your main target:

- maximum speed
- minimal strength and durability
- minimal running cost
- minimal construction cost and time
- maximum safety and comfort.

Record and discuss your initial ideas and then as a group, design and make a device which achieves the best possible balance between all performance targets.

# Legoids

People tend to use one of two main ways of moving around – two legs, or wheels.

Two legs give a human being just the right balance of speed, agility and control, but for a machine four, six, or surprisingly enough one leg can be more effective.

The wheel is an excellent invention for movement along flat surfaces, but only a small proportion of the earth is covered by roadways, which have to be specially built. The rest is sand, earth, rocks, and water.

**ASSIGNMENT**

Find out about some of the ways in which insects, birds, animals and fish move. Using a construction kit, build a working model of a machine which 'walks'. To help give you some initial ideas, look closely at the ways in which clocks, static machines, mechanical toys and vehicles work.

- What tasks might the machine perform?
- What scale is the model?
- Can the model be computer controlled?

Produce an explanatory A3 sheet to explain your final design

This acceleration is graphically dramatized by a thumbnail account of the progress in transportation. It has been pointed out, for example, that in 6000 BC, the fastest transportation over long distances available to people was the camel caravan, averaging eight miles per hour. It was not until about 3000 BC, when the chariot was invented, that the maximum speed was raised to roughly 20 m.p.h. So impressive was this invention, so difficult was it to exceed this speed limit that nearly 5000 years later, when the first mail coach began operating in England in 1784, it averaged a mere ten m.p.h. The first steam locomotive, introduced in 1825, could muster a top speed of only 13 m.p.h., and the great sailing ships of the time laboured along at less than half that speed. It was probably not until the 1880s that humans, with the help of a more advanced steam locomotive, managed to reach a speed of 100 m.p.h. It took the human race millions of years to attain that record. It took only 50 years, however, to quadruple the limit; so that by 1931, airborne humans were cracking the 400-m.p.h. line. It took a mere 20 years to double the limit again. And by the 1960s, rocket planes approached speeds of 4000 m.p.h. and people in space capsules were circling the earth at 18 000 m.p.h. Plotted on a graph, the line representing progress in the past generation would leap vertically off the page.

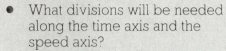

## ASSIGNMENT

Carefully read the passage on the left. Work in a group to produce a large-scale illustrated graph to show the relationship between time and the increasing speeds at which people have been able to travel.

- What divisions will be needed along the time axis and the speed axis?
- How big will the graph need to be to adequately display the increases in the past fifty years?
- Where can the final graph be displayed?

# Clothing

Clothes have always served two purposes. Early humans used animal skins to provide protection from the elements – cold, wind or heat, but also for tribal and personal identification, and ritual decoration.

Now there is an extensive range of natural and synthetic fibres, and computerized production lines to make our garments, but we still use our clothes for the same two basic reasons.

Well-designed clothing will not only fit well and provide the desired protection but will also make the wearer feel comfortable and self-confident.

Choosing which clothes to buy, and which to wear together, are important everyday design decisions we all have to make.

Nowadays many of the jobs we do require us to wear clothing which will protect us from much more than the weather. Industrial processes can expose workers to toxic fumes and extremes of heat, cold and damp. People who undertake potentially dangerous physical activities – stunt artists, sportsmen and women, etc., also need to wear protective clothing. And in some situations, such as hospitals, food preparation and microelectronics, special garments are needed to keep the environment free of the minute skin particles, hair and fabric fibres which we all unknowingly shed every day.

Other important jobs require people to wear uniforms, partly for functional purposes, but mostly so that they can be instantly recognized as a traffic warden, clown, school pupil, or whatever.

Strangely enough people often take unnecessary risks and do not bother to wear the protective clothing which is available. It is therefore important that such garments are carefully and individually designed to:
- provide the necessary protection
- fit comfortably
- assist the wearer to do his or her job
- be easy to put on and take off
- look attractive.

In the future remote-controlled machines will increasingly remove the need for people to work in very dangerous situations, making some types of protective clothing no longer necessary. Most accidents happen in ordinary, everyday situations, however, and there is still plenty of scope for the design of simple protective clothing which people will be happy to wear.

## DISCUSSION ISSUES
- Is fashion important?
- Are synthetic materials preferable to natural materials?

# Clothes sense

Make a list of six different items of clothing you possess. Make a simple coloured sketch of each, stating all the different components (fabrics, materials, buttons, zips, etc.) it is made from. Include your answers to the following questions about each garment:
- What does it feel like?
- What does it sound like?
- What does it look like?

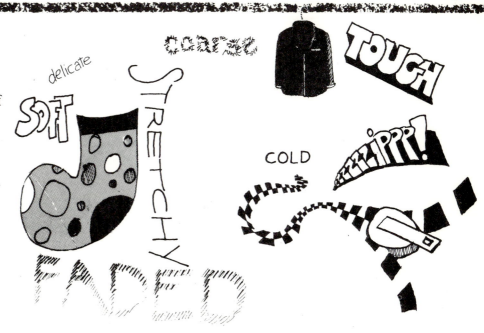

## Fit for the job

### Cover up
Make a list of all the people you can think of who wear special clothes designed for the job or task they do. Try and think of at least fifty.

Organize your list into groups under the following headings:
- sport
- entertainment
- identity
- work
- military.

Don't worry if some items could fit into more than one list.

Select two or three examples from each category and produce an A3 presentation sheet illustrated with sketches, pictures cut from magazines or photocopied images.

### Made to measure
Talk to someone you know who wears a uniform or protective clothing of some sort.
- Why is it designed and made the way it is?
- What materials is it made from?
- How well does it fit?
- What does the wearer think of it?

Sketch the garment and take some accurate overall measurements, such as sleeve length, chest size, etc. Work up coloured scale drawings of the back and front of the garment, or choose other appropriate views.

### Fancy dress
Design a uniform or protective clothing for someone who works:
- in a chocolate factory
- selling ice-creams and hot-dogs
- as a lion-tamer
- as a 'lollipop' man or woman.

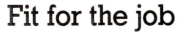

# Off the peg (1)

## Investigation ✎

Write a list of all the items which are part of your present school uniform – blazer, particular coloured socks, sports outfits, etc.

Think carefully and make a note of the three things you dislike most about any items of your school uniform – its colours, use, style maybe?

Working in a group put together a short questionnaire to discover what other people in your class and year think about the uniform. If they could choose their own uniform what alternatives can they suggest which they would like to wear? Ask some younger and older members of the school as well to see if their opinions and ideas differ.

Identify which of your teachers are very strict about how you wear your uniform, and those who don't seem to mind too much. Explain to them what your assignment is and ask them why they think school uniform is or isn't important.

Boy, well-to-do family 1880's

Schoolgirls in gymslips 1917

## First thoughts 💡

Taking close account of the information you have discovered from your investigation, sketch ideas for **three** different ranges of possible new school uniforms. The garments may be completely new designs of your own, or closely based on existing items of clothing.

Your designs for each range must:
- include co-ordinating colours and/or patterns
- contain outdoor garments to keep you warm and dry in winter
- include provision for carrying everyday items – pens, combs, bus-pass, etc.

Some of your ideas should be fairly conventional, whereas others will involve much more inventive approaches. Think about how each garment could be made, and how much it might cost.

For each range also design and draw up a new school badge, to help co-ordinate the uniform and sports-wear. It should be as simple and visual as possible.

Badge

Black, navy or white shirt for years 1-3. 4&5 can wear any colour

SLGS

Badge to be sewn onto shirt, jumper, track-suit top + shirt

Games shorts cotton for comfort and hygeine

Navy, Blue or Black skirt or trousers can be worn

OFF THE PEG FINAL PRESENTATION

# Off the peg (2)

## Developing ideas

Produce an A4 or A3 presentation in colour of each of your three possible ranges.

Undertake a further survey by showing your presentations to a number of people and recording which range they liked best and any other relevant comments they made.

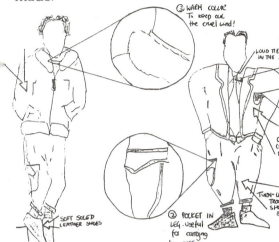

## Realization

When you have completed your survey decide which range of your designs are going to be the most popular and acceptable. Obtain some fabric samples, and maybe make a mock-up garment.

Your final task is to take your designs to your head teacher and see if you can interest him or her in changing the school uniform.

You will have to prepare for this very carefully. Start by seeing the school secretary to make a proper appointment.

Plan out what you are each going to say, what you will show him or her, and when.

You will need to explain about your project as a whole, and to provide the results of your initial research. Will it be a good idea to show the two rejected ranges as well as the one you finally chose?

If necessary you may have to re-present your research work and the final presentation drawings.

Summer Uniform    Winter Uniform    Sports Items

## Evaluation

After your interview with the head, write up in full what happened.

- Did he or she understand the points you were making?
- To what extent did you agree with any critical comments which were made?

## Further development

Imagine that the assignment is about to be passed on to someone else to complete. Make a series of recommendations as to how you think things will need to proceed:

- How might the designs be generally improved?
- What will need to be discovered about manufacturing processes and costs?
- What range of sizes will each item need to be made available in?

# Roboritual (1)

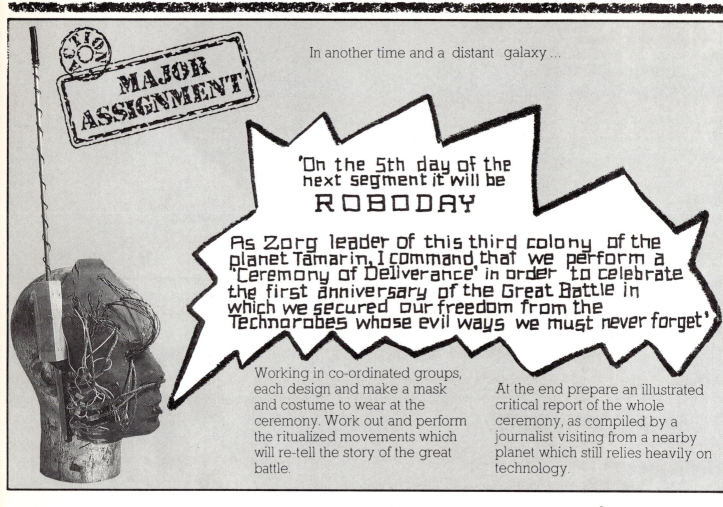

MAJOR ASSIGNMENT

In another time and a distant galaxy ...

'On the 5th day of the next segment it will be

**ROBODAY**

As Zorg leader of this third colony of the planet Tamarin, I command that we perform a 'Ceremony of Deliverance' in order to celebrate the first anniversary of the Great Battle in which we secured our freedom from the Technorobes whose evil ways we must never forget'

Working in co-ordinated groups, each design and make a mask and costume to wear at the ceremony. Work out and perform the ritualized movements which will re-tell the story of the great battle.

At the end prepare an illustrated critical report of the whole ceremony, as compiled by a journalist visiting from a nearby planet which still relies heavily on technology.

## What is a ritual?

**Rituals**, or **ceremonies**, are sequences of events which are always performed in the same way – like dancing round a maypole, morning assembly, or even eating Sunday lunch!

They are important occasions because they help provide a sense of order and permanence – something that stays the same in an ever-changing world.

Many ancient rituals serve to remind us of our common past, and give us a sense of our history. Others are superstitious, and are performed to bring us good fortune, or to fend off evil spirits.

## Planning the ritual

Working in groups, suggest roles for each character, based on the masks which have been made.
- How could simple costumes be made to go with the masks?
- How can the movements be 'scored'?

How did the Technorobes move?

What sounds did they make?

What was so bad about the Technorobes?

How were they defeated?

What technology does the planet still rely on?

**Masks** are artificial faces worn for protection or disguise. As a disguise a mask might be used to help avoid being recognized, or serve to exaggerate the expressions of the face in a performance of some sort.

## Investigation

Start by making a list of all the different occasions when someone might need to wear a mask of some sort. Try and think of at least twenty. Using pictures cut from magazines, photocopies and your own drawings, make a large collage sheet of various masks.

Look particularly at any modern protective masks or helmets which incorporate devices such as breathing apparatus, communication systems, etc.

# Roboritual (2)

Working in groups study the collage sheets and discuss the effectiveness of each mask.

- Why has it been designed the way it has?
- How well does it work?
- How might it have been made?
- How much would it have cost?
- Does it look comfortable to wear?

## Masks

| Protection | Disguise |
|---|---|
| Sea divers | Actors |
| Sportsmen | Highwaymen |
| Knights | Witches |
| Spacemen | |

## First thoughts 💡

Using the lists of masks and collage sheets for reference, draw a series of rough sketches of lots of different initial ideas for a robotic-type mask. Experiment with various combinations of practical and visual features.

Start to make a collection of possible materials for later use – string, coloured wires, discarded electrical components and so on. Some of them may well give you ideas for your design.

Look back through your ideas and select the best ones.

- Which will be easiest to make?
- Which will be most effective?

*continued ...*

# Roboritual (3)

## Developing ideas ◎

Use further sketches to explore what happens if you change different parts of your chosen design by:

- moving them to different places
- adding further components
- removing features
- using different materials
- changing the colours and textures.

Work out exactly how the mask will be made:

- What will the basic structure be?
- Which parts will need to be specially made?
- What 'ready-made' materials can be used?
- How can the various components be joined together?

# Roboritual (4)

## Realization ♛

When you have finalized your
ideas, prepare a neat working
drawing and make your mask.
Plan out carefully the order in
which you will make it – don't
forget you can always be getting
on with a different part while the
glue or paint is drying on another.

As you work you may spot
improvements you can make.
Discuss your ideas with others in
your group. Get someone to try on
the mask so that you can check
that all is going well.

Diary
'The main part of
the mask was made
from an old welding
mask my Dad gave me.
The hearing systems
were made out of
old spray paint lids.

The centre piece is
a video-camera made
out of a soda stream
gas bottle top and
another spray paint
lid.'

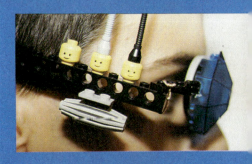
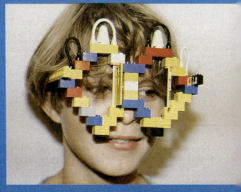

# Any colour you like (2)

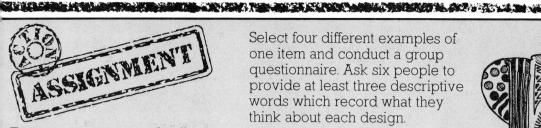

**ASSIGNMENT**

Twenty years ago nearly all jerseys, ties, shirts, shorts and socks were very plain. Today though, there are hundreds of different designs and colours to choose from.

Produce designs for yourself for any one of the items listed above which you could wear to one of the following events:
- a halloween or bonfire night party
- a disco
- some other specific event or occasion of your own choice.

Make a collection of magazine cuttings, sketches, etc., to show the variety of designs now available.

Select four different examples of one item and conduct a group questionnaire. Ask six people to provide at least three descriptive words which record what they think about each design.

### First thoughts 💡
Produce a series of sketch designs to explore several different possible approaches, and a range of variations of patterns, textures and colour combinations. Identify which you think are the best ideas, and why.

### Realization 🖐
Using large sheets of paper, draw out and colour a full-size representation of your final design. If you can, obtain an old white T-shirt, pair of socks or shorts or a shirt and transfer the design onto it using fabric dyes and/or odd fabric remnants.

# Fantastic hats

**ASSIGNMENT**

Until quite recently hats were very common everyday objects worn by almost everybody. Wearing an unusual hat was a good way of creating a distinctive personal image.
- Why do people wear hats?
- How many different sorts of hats are there?

Identify and illustrate:
- five famous people (real or fictional) who always wear particular, very distinctive hats
- five situations in which hats are worn for protective, rather than decorative purposes
- five ceremonial or ritual occasions when hats, or head-coverings of some sort, are used.

Ask your grandparents or other elderly relatives to tell you about some of the hats they used to wear, or can remember other people wearing.

Sketch ideas for **three** fantastic hats. One should be for yourself, another for a particular famous person, and one based on a theme of your choice – animals, birds, food, for example.

Select the best idea for further development. If you are going to make a final version you will have to think carefully about whether you can obtain and work the materials you would need.

You should then make a small model in three dimensions, using Plasticine or clay. Next make a full-size prototype from thin card, shaping and bending it round someone's head, before proceeding to the final construction.

# Food

The production and consumption of food and drink has always been a human preoccupation. Over the centuries machines and devices have transformed the way we grow, harvest, catch, store and prepare the food we eat every day. Today we can have almost any item of food we want, at any time of the year, and at a reasonable price.

The human body has often been compared with a machine, as both require fuel (food) as energy to run on. But people also need food to supply essential substances, called **nutrients**, for body-building, protection and maintenance.

A variety of different nutrients are required – a complex mixture of **sugar, starch** and **fats** for daily energy, **protein** for body-building, and **vitamins** and **minerals** for protection.

Each item of food, or each combination of foods in a meal, contains a different mixture of nutrients. So we need to eat a variety of different things to ensure we obtain the correct balance we need to work efficiently – and keep healthy.

Food is important to us in other ways, too. We have established many myths, traditions, rituals and events based on eating and drinking – bobbing for apples at halloween, harvest festival, dinner parties, celebratory banquets and so on. So food needs to be enjoyable as well as good for us.

Today there is a much greater variety of food available which is quick and easy to prepare, looks appetising, and usually tastes good too. But our diet is often not as healthy as it could be. This is because it frequently does not contain the right sort of balance of the different nutrients we need. Some foods contain chemicals which may have unexpected and unpleasant side-effects. And nowadays we are often encouraged by advertisements and social situations to eat and drink more than we really need to.

*There is an old saying 'You are what you eat'.*

## DISCUSSION ISSUES

- How could people be encouraged to eat a better balanced diet?
- Should 'fast food' be highly taxed?
- What food should be available for school dinners?

# Rational diets

What did people eat during the last war? Ask older friends and relatives what they can remember about their diet during that time. Perhaps they even have an old ration book you could see.

Draw a picture of a table top which shows the full range and typical amount of food eaten in a week during war-time. How nutritionally well balanced does it appear to be?

Make a list of all the food you eat in a typical week using the headings **meat**, **vegetable**, **fruit**, **sweet**. Draw a picture of another table top to illustrate how much you consume.

# Gastronomic guesswork

What are your three favourite dishes? Write down a description of each, but without actually naming them.
- What colour is it?
- What shape is it?
- How does it feel?
- What does it taste like?
- Is it expensive?
- How is it made?

Read your descriptions out to someone else and see how many clues you have to give them before they can guess what it is.

# Designer spells

Imagine you are a witch or a wizard. A client has asked you to prepare a potion to cure one of the following ailments:
- spots before the eyes
- stomach-ache
- hairy feet
- coughs and sneezes.

Choose six suitable strange and scary but just edible ingredients to put into the magic brew. How many and how much of each will you need? Under no circumstances should you test your ideas out!

Write the final recipe out as a spell to be chanted out, complete with illustrations, to include in your shortly-to-be-published cookbook.

You decide to mass-produce and market your potion.

Design an eye-catching, spine-tingling poster to advertise it.

Spell book

Take a fresh green leek
and some bubble & squeak

A strawberry cake and
a piece of steak

Mix them all up with
the garden rake

# Back to nature (1)

A new chain of small health-food restaurants and take-aways is planning to open across the country.

Choose a suitable brand name for the company, and design a simple logo or symbol to visually co-ordinate its products and services.

Work in a group of about four. Agree to adopt the name and logo thought out by one of the group, and divide the following tasks up amongst yourselves. Make sure you keep a careful record of what you do.

Work in rough to begin with. Remember to always consider several possibilities for each task and discuss your ideas with the other members of your group before coming to any final decisions.

Towards the end of the project you should each prepare final coloured presentation sheets of your ideas. Imagine your proposals are to be sent to the company for consideration, so they will need to be completely self-explanatory, and give the **reasons** for your decisions.

Make a collection of pictures cut from magazines, photocopies and sketches of animals, and food which is in its natural state – fruit, vegetables and so on. Assemble them together in a collage entitled **Back to nature**.

Create a design which can be printed onto their range of recycled paper cups, plates and napkins.

Prepare an illustrated menu to show the things which are available to eat in or take away. Include details of the nutritional value and composition of each dish.

Make a list of the various jobs which will be created by the new company. Choose two different jobs and write out what qualifications and qualities a prospective applicant is likely to need.

Design a uniform to be worn by staff serving in the restaurant.

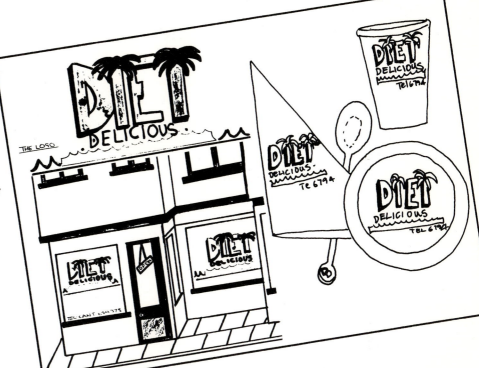

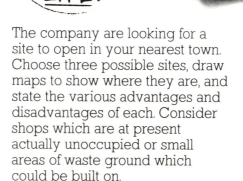

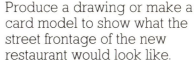

The company are looking for a site to open in your nearest town. Choose three possible sites, draw maps to show where they are, and state the various advantages and disadvantages of each. Consider shops which are at present actually unoccupied or small areas of waste ground which could be built on.

- Is the size right?
- Is it in a good position to attract passers-by?
- Is there any parking space?
- Is anyone likely to complain?

Decide which you think the best site is, giving the reasons for your choice.

Produce a drawing or make a card model to show what the street frontage of the new restaurant would look like.

Make up a fifteen-second advertising jingle to be played on your local commercial radio station the week before a restaurant opens.

What special offer could be made to encourage the public to attend on the opening day?

Which famous personality would you invite to open the restaurant? Can you think of any simple publicity stunts which could be set up?

# Fast food

Make a collection of fun-food wrappers and advertisements which contain drawings (not photographs) of food. Look very closely at the way each illustration has been done.

- Which media have been used?
- How has texture been represented?
- Has it been simplified?
- Has it been exaggerated in any way?

Using various combinations of different coloured pens, pencils and paints, experiment to discover effective ways of representing food graphically. Record for each which media you used, how long it took and how successful you think it is.

In rough, write a list of ingredients for an imaginary dream 'jumbo'-sized hamburger, pizza or ice-cream sundae. Sketch out a plan and elevation of your creation, and work out how to best use colours and textures to represent each ingredient. Try to make your illustration as mouth-watering and irresistible as you can by exaggerating its lusciousness and sickliness.

Very neatly draw up the final presentation, and carefully work up the colours and textures.

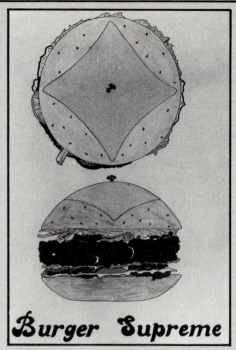

*Burger Supreme*

Make a list of words used to describe food which include the following sounds:
oo/ee/zz/ss/ch
For example, 'fizzy', 'gooey', 'crunchy', etc. Invent some new taste words using similar sounds.

Think of a suitable name for your dream dish and label the ingredients with original 'taste' words. Experiment with designs for a suitable style of lettering. Carefully choose the right height and width of lettering to go with your illustration, and add a title to the final presentation.

Using PVA, Plasticine, foam and/or other materials make three-dimensional models of your creations.

# Sandwich survey

Working in a group undertake a survey to discover:
- which local shops offer the best pre-packed sandwiches?
- what are people's favourite fillings?

Each group member should visit one shop, and ask to speak to someone in charge.

What is the best way of finding out people's favourite fillings? Conclude your survey with a clear statement of which six varieties you would recommend a shop to make.

- When are the sandwiches made and packed?
- When are they put onto the shelves?
- When are they taken off the shelves if unsold?

- What range of fillings do they stock?
- How much do they cost?
- How good is the packaging?

# Guess who's coming to the party?

As a group you are planning a party, and each of you is inviting a suprise guest who will be one of the following:
- a film star (past or present)
- a notorious historical person
- a fictional character.

Carefully select the particular person you intend to invite, but keep his or her identity a secret. Choose some appropriate party games they might like to play, and plan what food you should supply, which should be as outrageous and inventive as possible. Using appropriate modelling materials (but **not** real food) create one of the dishes you have thought up, placed on a cardboard plate.

Design and make some suitable cutlery for your guest, along with a paper hat.

Set up a long table with a place-setting and meal for each of your group's guests, and a list of party games. See if you can each work out who's coming to the party!

# Design and society

As we have seen, people have come to depend on products, places and communications which have been designed to help them through their daily lives. Good design is needed to achieve a balance between what we need and want, and what technology can provide.

But is everything right with the world?

*Earthrise*

'It's so incredibly impressive when you look back at our planet from out there in space and you realize so forcibly that it's a closed system – that we don't have any unlimited resources, that there's only so much air and so much water.'
Ed Mitchell, Apollo 14 Astronaut

## Spaceship Earth (1)

A system is a collection of different parts which are connected in some way. All the parts are finely balanced. Changing one part has an effect on all the other parts.

There are many different sorts of system, each in turn forming one of the parts of a larger system. They can be large or small, simple or complex, open or closed. A closed system is one which is completely self-contained.

The desert island you were stranded on at the start of this book could be thought of as a closed system with limited resources. A spaceship would be another example of a self-contained system of products, places, communications and people which interact together to enable the craft to fly through space over an extended period of time.

In many ways Planet Earth is like a spaceship. Our **supplies**, the things we need to survive our journey around the Sun, are already on board – the air to breathe, food and water to eat and drink, and raw materials to make things from. The only external source of energy is light from the Sun itself.

Our sophisticated life-support system is capable of replenishing itself, but it can only do so successfully if a very delicate natural balance is maintained between living things and the air, water and minerals. People are an intricate part of this system, and must contribute to it as well as depending on it.

On the Spaceship Earth flight control deck, a number of critical warning lights have recently started flashing. The first indicates that there is now an alarming **population growth** across the planet, so there are now many more people to support. Unfortunately another light shows that not only are we using our **supplies** up more quickly than nature can replace them, but also that many of them are being **polluted** – poisoned and destroyed by ourselves.

And yet another flashing light reminds us that the system has suddenly started to **change** more rapidly than people can adequately cope with. What is perhaps most alarming of all though, is that most people seem to be completely ignoring the warning signs.

## Population

On Spaceship Earth there is only a limited amount of land to support life. Until recently, famine and disease meant that the number of people on board could easily be looked after.

Now, through improved health care and intensive farming methods, technological capability enables people to live longer. At present the population is doubling in size every forty years. The extra people need extra space, and have had to start to move further across the land, decreasing the amount available for food production. And the problem with intensive farming methods is that they are only a short-term solution which eventually destroys the land.

*Rainforest clearance for agriculture, Australia*

## Energy matters

The manufacture and operation of modern technology relies primarily on the use of **fossil fuels** – oil, coal and natural gas. These fuels supply energy originally drawn from the Sun and stored beneath the surface of the Earth over millions of years. Roughly every 24 hours we use up resources which have taken 1000 years to form. At the present rate fossil fuels are expected to run out during the next century.

In such circumstances it is suprising to realize that a high proportion of the energy resources we draw on is **wasted**. One important approach to our problems is therefore to try and persuade people to **save** precious energy whenever possible.

## Pollution

Many of the machines and devices which provide us with the everyday things we need and want produce unfortunate side-effects, polluting the atmosphere, environment and water with poisonous waste chemicals, litter and noise. Increasing areas of land are now no longer suitable for growing food. Some lakes and rivers are unable to support fish.

There has also been a sudden increase in the amount of **carbon dioxide** in the atmosphere. This has been caused mainly by:
- the extensive burning of fossil fuels
- the use of oxygen in manufacturing processes
- the destruction of large areas of forests, which play an essential part in the replenishment cycle.

The result of these factors is often called the **greenhouse effect**. Eventually the temperature of the atmosphere could increase to the point where the polar ice-caps melt, causing the water level across the world to rise dramatically. At the same time the **ozone layer**, which protects us from certain harmful sun rays, is being worn away.

All these things will eventually destroy the careful balance of natural systems of replenishment. Even space itself has come to be used as a waste tip for used-up satellites and spacecraft.

*Hardwood logs from tropical rainforest*

*continued …*

# Spaceship Earth (3)

## Alternatives?

During the last fifteen years there has been an increase in research and development into alternative sources of energy. The main possibilities are:

- wind power
- tidal/wave power
- solar energy
- geothermal power
- biomass
- nuclear power.

At present none of these approaches has been sufficiently developed to provide a realistic alternative source of energy. It seems extremely unlikely that anyone will discover a new miracle power source in the immediate future. For now, saving energy would seem to be the best approach.

## Dealing with change

Few things in life are certain. One is that the future will be different. Change is a natural and inevitable event. Technology is the major source of change in society.

Up to now technological change has been relatively slow, at a rate which people can accept and adjust to. Recently though technological capability has developed at an amazing speed which has left many people feeling bewildered, overwhelmed and threatened by inventions they are unable to understand or control. The mind converts mental stress into physical illness. Rather like the Earth, the human–biological system is under strain, and liable to break down.

*Electricity wind turbines, California*

*Detergent in stream, Kenya*

## Changing attitudes to technology

Earlier this century everyone tended to believe that technology was a wonderful thing, capable of solving all the world's problems. During the past twenty years or so, however, many people's attitudes towards technological change have altered as they have become more aware of the potential disadvantages that there seem to be.

Perhaps the greatest problem is **people** themselves. It is relatively easy to tackle a technical problem, like going to the moon and back – all it takes is time, money and brainpower. Technology can help people live longer and more comfortably, but it can't change the way they think and act.

If we are to continue to survive on a long-term basis we urgently need to develop new attitudes towards the longer-term use of our basic life-support systems. We need to put a much higher value on the way we care for our real needs, and the natural environment we live in.

Clearly there are no right or wrong answers to these questions, but they represent issues and concerns which underlie many of the everyday decisions which people make, and will continue to make in the future.

In these final assignments, you will be considering different ways in which those important changes in attitudes and values might start to be brought about. Of all the activities in this book, these are the ones which matter the most.

Spaceship Earth still has a great deal further to travel. We all need to remember that it is not ours to keep and throw away it has only been borrowed from future generations.

### Recycled information

Design a poster which visually presents the answer to **one** of the following questions.

- How fast is the world population growing?
- In which years is each fossil fuel presently likely to run out?
- In what ways do we commonly waste energy?
- How do each of the alternative approaches to providing energy work?
- What are the difficulties and disadvantages of each approach?
- In what circumstances does modern technological change cause stress?

# A campaign of action

Devise a way of doing something which will actively help to restore the balance of nature. Don't expect to save the world on your own, just remember that every little bit will help. Your project might involve:

- increasing the awareness of other people to the seriousness of the situation, and what needs to be done
- raising money for charitable organizations concerned with environmental problems
- saving everyday energy
- producing less carbon dioxide or other pollutants.

Working individually or in small groups decide which activity you are going to tackle. Discuss the possible ways in which you could achieve your objective. Finalize your plan of action, making sure you keep a record of what you have decided to do, and why.

If you haven't already done so, you will probably need to obtain some relevant factual information on the problem you are dealing with.

At the end of the project you must be able to provide clear **evidence** of what you have achieved – figures and statements which demonstrate how much energy you saved, the amount of pollution you reduced, how people's attitudes and opinions have begun to change.

'We started by devising a questionnaire to discover how much our friends and neighbours were aware of the pollution which results from using petrol with lead in. We also found out how difficult or not it was for the motorist to obtain and use lead-free petrol.

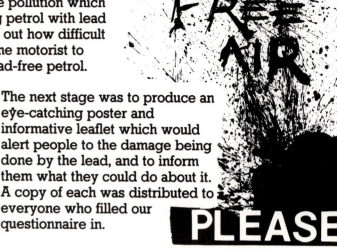

The next stage was to produce an eye-catching poster and informative leaflet which would alert people to the damage being done by the lead, and to inform them what they could do about it. A copy of each was distributed to everyone who filled our questionnaire in.

After a week we asked them to fill in a second copy of the questionnaire, and produced comparative graphs to show how their understanding of the situation had improved. In our final report we also included some of the general comments people made, together with the good news that two motorists were now in the process of having their cars fitted to run on lead-free petrol.'

'We wrote a short play set in the future just before each of the world's resources were due to run out. We each played the part of a resource and designed and made appropriate costumes for ourselves to wear as we explained to the audience how we had been misused. An adult helped organize some performance-spaces for us, and at the end of each a collection was taken. Eventually we were able to donate £20 to a conservation charity.'

'I calculated how much electricity we used each day lighting our home. I explained to everyone how much fuel, and money, was wasted by leaving lights on when they were not really necessary. With my help and encouragement we were able to save 20% of our electricity consumption for lighting.'

Design a small family house for the early part of next century. Make energy conservation an important consideration. Your ideas should not be too fantastic – humanoid robots and matter transference machines are for a lot further into the future.

- Will the house be above or below ground?
- Which way will it face?
- What materials would be best?
- What overall shape could it be?
- What would the doors and windows be like?
- How would the interior be divided up?
- What would the inside and outside look like?
- What fuels and devices might be used for cooking and heating?
- How will its occupants feel about living there? What will be the main advantages and the disadvantages?

Concentrate on any two rooms in the house. Draw up a series of colourful plans and elevations, supported by a full written description explaining why you have designed the rooms the way you have.

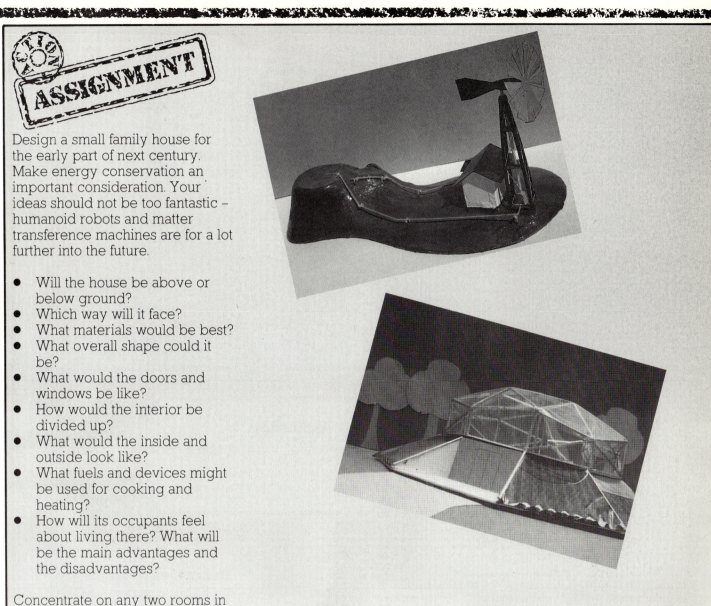

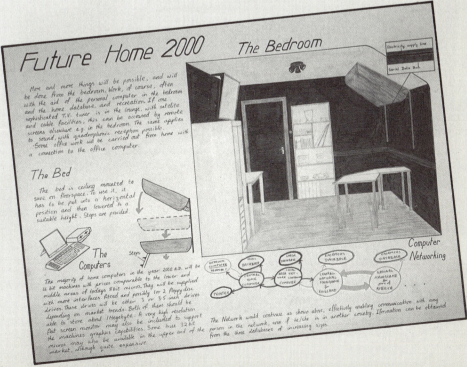

# Moonbase: a giant leap for mankind? (1)

If we had the opportunity to start afresh, what would we do? This final assignment will provide you with the opportunity to speculate about the sort of future world you might ideally like to live in.

Think back over all the activities you have undertaken from this book, and remember all the various advantages and disadvantages you discovered about the way we use technology at present.

It is the year 2020. A Moonbase is being established, and designs for the first Space City are now being considered. The city will be multi-national, and its main purpose will be the large-scale manufacture of certain chemicals and other products which can only be made in zero-gravity conditions. There will also be a large telecommunications centre for monitoring and relaying information across the Earth.

The city will have to cater for all the needs of the people who will be expected to settle there on a mainly permanent basis. Initially 500 people will start the community, to be followed by further groups of 500 every six months until there is a population of 5000.

Working in a group, imagine you have been asked to make a series of proposals about the way the city should be designed and organized. Your ideas should be presented in the form of visual illustrations, models and written material, or maybe through a performance of some sort.

## Starting points
Consider a broad range of the following starting questions. Choose one main topic area to develop some detailed proposals. Some research will probably be needed to discover more about the atmospheric and gravitational conditions of the Moon.

## Fair exchange
- How will people be rewarded for the work they do?
- Will there need to be any advertising and marketing?

## Design and society
- What resources are there on the Moon which can be used?
- To what extent can the city be self-sufficient?
- Will energy be brought from the Earth?
- Will the balance of nature need to be replicated?
- What Earth rituals and traditions will be retained? What new ones will be needed?

## Transport
- In what circumstances will people need to travel around and to explore?
- What will be the most important considerations – speed, comfort, safety, cost?

## Work, rest and play
- Apart from manufacturing and communications, what other 'service' industries will there need to be?
- How will the working day be organized?
- What leisure activities will be provided?

## Everyday objects
- What new tools and appliances might be needed?
- What would they do?
- What would they look like?
- What existing items will be brought from Earth?

### Shelter
- Where on the Moon will the base be?
- What elements will settlers need to be protected from?
- What structures and materials will be most suitable?
- How will energy for heating and lighting be supplied?
- How will the living quarters be arranged?
- What public facilities will be needed?
- Where will they be located in the city?

### Food
- What will people eat and drink?
- Where will it come from?
- How will it be prepared and served?

### Clothing
- What protective garments will be needed?
- What might styles and fashions be like?

### Information
- What kind of communication and information retrieval and storage devices will be needed?
- How will people be encouraged and persuaded to want to go to live on the Moon?

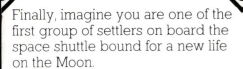

Finally, imagine you are one of the first group of settlers on board the space shuttle bound for a new life on the Moon.

... You are sitting in the aircraft-style passenger accommodation. There is a sense of motionlessness as you glide through space towards the Moon. The steady hum of the rocket motors and air-conditioning systems provides a constant background. Everything seems new, clean and efficient.

Through the port-hole window there is little to be seen – all is dark and quiet. Look ahead and see the cold unwelcoming face of the Moon, getting larger and larger. Behind you the Earth is still large on the horizon, and you can easily make out the major continents and oceans.

Settle back in your comfortable chair, and pause for thought:
- What will it feel like to live on the Moon?
- What are you looking forward to?
- Why did you decide to go?
- What will it be good to get away from?
- What things will you miss the most?
- What do you hope for the most?
- How will you best be able to contribute to the future survival of the Earth?

# Index

advertising 45–6, 52, 89
airport survival kit 85
asking questions 7, 9
axonometric drawing 66, 70

board game 60–61
bus station 82–3

ceremony 23, 30–1, 92
city
    centre community 32–3
    planning 33, 110–11
clothing 6, 21, 88–97
    accessories 96–7
    ceremonial 92–5
    colour 96–7
    function 88–91
    hats 96–7
coding systems 77
communications 26–7, 73–9, 109
    breakdown 77
    evaluation 73
    telepathic 77
community 6, 24, 28–33
containers 34, 37, 85

design 5
    history 32, 34–5, 40, 45, 72, 87, 90
    skills 7–16
    and society 21, 104–11
    survival of objects 40
developing ideas 7, 10–11
diet 98, 99

Earth 105–6
emotional response 6, 37–8
employment 54
energy 105, 106
    conservation 109
environmental evaluation 29
ergonomics 35
evaluation 8
everyday objects 21, 26–7, 37
exchange 6, 24, 44–52, 111
exhibition 25
extenders 34

food 6, 22, 98–103, 110–11
    fast 102
fun machines 58
furniture 42, 70

games 31, 60–1

hats 96–7
health-food chain 100–1
holiday transport 84
homes 27, 62–71
house design 63–71, 109

illustrations 15
imagination 7, 16–7
information 24, 72–9, 110–1
information matrix/net 82–3
initiative 4
inventions 41
investigation 7, 9
island, survival on 18–25

layout 15
leisure 6, 54
lettering 14
locomotion 85, 86
logos 78–9

magic ritual 23, 92
marketing 44, 47, 52, 99
masks 92–5
mechanical movement 56–7, 59, 86
media 25, 46
messages 24, 75, 76, 77
Mickey Mouse 103
moonbase 110–11
musical instruments 23

nutrients 98

organisation
    work 7, 13
    page layout 14

party planning 103
person, parts of 5
personal stereos 47–51
personalisation 64
places and spaces 26–7, 28–33
planning, work 7, 13
    see also city planning and town
        planning
play 2, 23, 31, 53, 59, 60–1
playgrounds 30–1, 58
pollution 105
population 105
presentation 7, 14–15
primary function 42–3
products 26–7, 34–5
    aesthetic response 37–8
    analysis and assessment 36, 39, 48
    survival 40
    uses 42–43
project
    diary 7
    report 14
promotion, advertising 45
protective clothing 88–9, 97
prototypes 7, 10–11
public transport 81, 82–3

questionnaires 49

realization 7, 12
recipe 99
rescue 25
resources 13
rest 6, 23, 53, 110–11
ritual
    clothing 92–5, 97
    magic 23
robots 55, 56–7, 92–5

sandwiches 103
schoolscapes 30–1
secondary function 42–3
shelter 6, 24, 62–71, 110–11
shipwreck 16–25
sketches 15
society and design 104–11
speed, transport 87
surreal fashion 96
survival 6, 20–5
symbols 78–9
systems 104
    coding 77
    life support 6, 104
    transport 82

technology 5, 6
    changes in 106–7
tertiary function 42–3
time organisation 13
titles 14
tools 24, 34
town planning 33, 71
toys 23, 59
transport 80–7, 110–11
typography 14

uniforms 88–9, 100
    school 90–1
utensils 24, 34

water 22
work 6, 23, 53–7, 110–11

95